Creating Community-Responsive Physicians

Concepts and Models
for Service-Learning
in **Medical Education**

Sarena D. Seifer, Kris Hermanns, and Judy Lewis, volume editors

Edward Zlotkowski, series editor

A PUBLICATION OF THE

AMERICAN ASSOCIATION
FOR HIGHER EDUCATION

Published in cooperation with Community-Campus Partnerships for Health

This monograph was published in cooperation with:

Community-Campus Partnerships for Health
3333 California Street, Suite 410
San Francisco, CA 94118
ph 415/476-7081, fax 415/476-4113
email ccph@itsa.ucsf.edu
http://futurehealth.ucsf.edu/ccph.html

Community-Campus
Partnerships for Health

Creating Community-Responsive Physicians: Concepts and Models for Service-Learning in Medical Education
(AAHE's Series on Service-Learning in the Disciplines)
Sarena D. Seifer, Kris Hermanns, and Judy Lewis, *volume editors*
Edward Zlotkowski, *series editor*

About This Publication
This volume is one of 18 in AAHE's Series on Service-Learning in the Disciplines. Additional copies of this publication, or others in the series from other disciplines, can be ordered using the form provided on the last page or by contacting:

AMERICAN ASSOCIATION FOR HIGHER EDUCATION
One Dupont Circle, Suite 360
Washington, DC 20036-1110
ph 202/293-6440 x780, fax 202/293-0073
www.aahe.org

ISBN 1-56377-014-8
ISBN (18 vol. set) 1-56377-005-9

Contents

About This Series
Edward Zlotkowski...v

Introduction
Sarena D. Seifer, Kris Hermanns, and Judy Lewis...1

*The Broader Context for Service-Learning
in Medical Education*

The Changing Health-Care System and Expectations of Physicians
Edward H. O'Neil...9

**Toward Building Communities of Commitment: Integrating
Community-Oriented Primary Care and Continuous Quality Improvement
Into Service-Learning**
Deborah Gardner, Andrew Schamess, Doreen Harper, and Denice Cora-Bramble.........................19

*Designing and Implementing
Service-Learning in Medical Education*

**Partners in Health Education:
Service-Learning by First-Year Medical Students**
Joseph F. Walsh, Jennifer Sage Smith, G. Christian Jernstedt,
Virginia A. Reed, and Sara Goodman 35

**Medical Students Go Back to Kindergarten:
Service-Learning and Medical Education in the Public Schools**
Kate Cauley, Elvira Jaballas, and Betty Holton...43

**Service-Learning in Medical Education: Teaching Psychiatry Residents
How to Work With the Homeless Mentally Ill**
Richard C. Christensen...55

**An Interdisciplinary Service-Learning Community Health Course
for Preclinical Health Sciences Students**
Daniel Blumenthal, Meryl S. McNeal, Lorine Spencer, JoAnne Rhone, and Fred Murphy..........63

**Service-Learning Opportunities at The Ohio State University:
The Community Medicine Rotation and the Community Project**
Franklin R. Banks and Catherine A. Heaney...69

**University of Connecticut School of Medicine:
An Urban Partnership**
Judy Lewis..77

**Initiating, Maintaining, and Sustaining
Community Partnerships: Developing Community-Based
Academic Health Professions Education Systems**
Bruce Bennard, Bruce Behringer, Carol Gentry, Mary Jane Kelley,
Paul E. Stanton, Jr., and Wanda Vaghan 91

**Integrating Teaching, Research, and Service at
East Tennessee State University: Action and Accountability
in Communities**
Joellen B. Edwards, Joy E. Wachs, Sheila M. Virgin, Bruce A. Goodrow,
and James E. Florence..103

**A Community Partnership in Service to the Homeless:
University of Pittsburgh and the City of Pittsburgh**
Thomas P. O'Toole, Joyce Holl, and Paul Freyder..115

**Student-Initiated Community Service:
The Community Health Advancement Program**
Sharon Dobie, Bonnie Beck, Melinda Tonelli, Charlene Forslund, Connie Huffine,
Deborah Kippen, Diane Staheli, and William Hobson 121

*Service-Learning Research
and Evaluation*

**The Socialization of Medical Students in a Preventive
Health Service-Learning Experience**
JoEllen Tarallo-Falk..131

**Evaluating the Impact of Service-Learning:
Applications for Medical Education**
Sherril B. Gelmon, Barbara Holland, Beth Morris, and Amy Driscoll..139

Appendix

Service-Learning Resources 157

Contributors to This Volume..177

About This Series

by Edward Zlotkowski

The following volume, *Creating Community-Responsive Physicians: Concepts and Models for Service-Learning in Medical Education,* represents the eighth in a series of monographs on service-learning and the academic disciplines. Ever since the early 1990s, educators interested in reconnecting higher education not only with neighboring communities but also with the American tradition of education for service have recognized the critical importance of winning faculty support for this work. Faculty, however, tend to define themselves and their responsibilities largely in terms of the academic disciplines/disciplinary areas in which they have been trained. Hence, the logic of the present series.

The idea for this series first surfaced late in 1994 at a meeting convened by Campus Compact to explore the feasibility of developing a national network of service-learning educators. At that meeting, it quickly became clear that some of those assembled saw the primary value of such a network in its ability to provide concrete resources to faculty working in or wishing to explore service-learning. Out of that meeting there developed, under the auspices of Campus Compact, a new national group of educators called the Invisible College, and it was within the Invisible College that the monograph project was first conceived. Indeed, a review of both the editors and contributors responsible for many of the volumes in this series would reveal significant representation by faculty associated with the Invisible College.

If Campus Compact helped supply the initial financial backing and impulse for the Invisible College and for this series, it was the American Association for Higher Education (AAHE) that made completion of the project feasible. Thanks to its reputation for innovative work, AAHE was not only able to obtain the funding needed to support the project up through actual publication, it was also able to assist in attracting many of the teacher-scholars who participated as writers and editors. AAHE is grateful also to the Corporation for National Service–Learn and Serve America for its financial support of the series.

Three individuals in particular deserve to be singled out for their contributions. Sandra Enos, former Campus Compact project director for Integrating Service With Academic Study, was shepherd to the Invisible College project. John Wallace, professor of philosophy at the University of Minnesota, was the driving force behind the creation of the Invisible College. Without his vision and faith in the possibility of such an undertaking, assembling the human resources needed for this series would have been very difficult.

Third, AAHE's endorsement — and all that followed in its wake — was due largely to then AAHE vice president Lou Albert. Lou's enthusiasm for the monograph project and his determination to see it adequately supported have been critical to its success. It is to Sandra, John, and Lou that the monograph series as a whole must be dedicated.

Another individual to whom the series owes a special note of thanks is Teresa E. Antonucci, who, as program manager for AAHE's Service-Learning Project, has helped facilitate much of the communication that has allowed the project to move forward.

The Rationale Behind the Series

A few words should be said at this point about the makeup of both the general series and the individual volumes. The idea of learning by doing is deeply rooted in modern medical education. From this standpoint, medical education might seem like a natural choice of disciplinary areas to include in this series. Natural fit has not, in fact, been a determinant factor in deciding which disciplines/interdisciplinary areas the series should include. Far more important have been considerations related to the overall range of disciplines represented. Since experience has shown that there is probably no disciplinary area — from architecture to zoology — where service-learning cannot be fruitfully employed to strengthen students' abilities to become active learners as well as responsible citizens, a primary goal in putting the series together has been to demonstrate this fact. Thus, some rather natural choices for inclusion — disciplines such as anthropology, geography, and religious studies — have been passed over in favor of other, sometimes less obvious selections from the business disciplines and natural sciences as well as several important interdisciplinary areas. Should the present series of volumes prove useful and well received, we can then consider filling in the many gaps we have left this first time around.

If a concern for variety has helped shape the series as a whole, a concern for legitimacy has been central to the design of the individual volumes. To this end, each volume has been both written by and aimed primarily at academics working in a particular disciplinary/interdisciplinary area. Many individual volumes have, in fact, been produced with the encouragement and active support of relevant discipline-specific national societies. For this volume, in fact, we owe thanks to Community-Campus Partnerships for Health.

Furthermore, each volume has been designed to include its own appropriate theoretical, pedagogical, and bibliographical material. Especially with regard to theoretical and bibliographical material, this design has resulted in considerable variation both in quantity and in level of discourse. Thus, for example, a volume such as Accounting contains more introductory and less bibliographical material than does Composition — simply because there is less written on and less familiarity with service-learning in accounting. However, no volume is meant to provide an extended introduction to service-learning *as a generic concept*. For material of this nature, the reader is referred to such texts as Kendall's *Combining Service and Learning: A Resource Book for Community and Public Service* (NSIEE, 1990) and Jacoby's *Service-Learning in Higher Education* (Jossey-Bass, 1996).

I would like to conclude with a note of special thanks to Sarena Seifer, Kris Hermanns, and Judy Lewis, coeditors of the present volume. In putting together a text that links health care for underserved populations with medical education reform, they have given us a work of more than academic significance.

February 1999

Introduction

by Sarena D. Seifer, Kris Hermanns, and Judy Lewis

Community-based education is a prominent theme across the health professions. No fewer than six national and international bodies have recently advocated expanding health professions education in community-based settings (Boelen 1992; Council on Graduate Medical Education 1995; Field 1995; Institute of Medicine 1988; Pew Health Professions Commission 1993; Schmidt et al. 1991). Leaders within academe have articulated a vision for community-based education based upon partnerships between health professions schools and the communities they serve (Bellack 1996; Cohen 1995; Foreman 1994; Sandoval 1996). These calls for curricular change are largely due to environmental factors, including changes in the financing and delivery of health care, changes in the financing of health professions education, concerns about the size, distribution, and quality of the health workforce, and the priorities of private grant makers.

Proponents of community-based health professions education advance numerous arguments for the important and unique learning opportunities offered in these settings (Barker 1990; Desjardins 1996; Faller et al. 1996; Feltovich et al. 1989; Lawrence 1988; Maurana and Goldenberg 1996; Smego and Costante 1996; Woolisscroft and Schwenk 1989). The leading ones include allowing learners to:

- Care for patients seen primarily in outpatient settings — especially patients who have chronic illnesses;
- Observe the natural and treated progression of diseases through continuity of care;
- Practice health promotion and disease prevention strategies;
- Develop patient communication and negotiation skills;
- Deal with social, financial, and ethical aspects of medical care;
- Increase students' capabilities and career interests in addressing the relevant health issues of rural and underserved communities.

Service-learning, an innovative form of education involving community partnerships, holds great promise as a curricular strategy for creating community-responsive physicians (Seifer 1998; Seifer, Connors, and O'Neil 1996).

It is important to recognize that service-learning, while a relatively new concept in health professions education, has its roots in undergraduate education. In 1982, Derek Bok of Harvard University described the social responsibilities of the modern university and the importance of shifting the locus of education and research to the community. In his landmark book *Scholarship Reconsidered*, Ernest Boyer (1990) contends that universities often overlook the potential for communities to contribute meaningfully to student education, research, and the development of knowledge. In addition to valuing the generation of knowledge (the traditional form of scholarship), he argues, higher education should also support the application of knowledge through faculty involvement in community outreach and community-based research. Over the past decade, there has been a growing movement within higher education to strengthen and further its traditional teaching, research, and service functions through community partnerships. This movement has been buoyed by such recent trends as demands for greater accountability on the part of publicly funded institutions and concerns over the relevance of the undergraduate curriculum in preparing graduates to be critical thinkers and engaged citizens. Service-learning has emerged as a curricular response to these trends (Jacoby 1996).

The considerable body of literature on service-learning contains literally hundreds of definitions of the term (Furco 1996). Taking common elements from these definitions, we define *service-learning* as a structured learning experience that combines community service with explicit learning objectives, preparation, and reflection. Students engaged in service-learning are expected not only to provide direct community service but also to learn about the context in which the service is provided, the connection between the service and their academic coursework, and their roles as citizens. Service-learning:

- Has its theoretical roots in experiential learning theory (Kolb 1984);
- Is developed, implemented, and evaluated in collaboration with the community;
- Responds to community-identified concerns;
- Attempts to balance the service that is provided and the learning that takes place;
- Enhances the curriculum by extending learning beyond the lecture hall and allowing students to apply what they are learning to real-world situations;
- Provides opportunities for critical reflection.

Service-Learning and Traditional Clinical Medical Education: Significant Differences

Service-learning differs from traditional clinical medical education in a number of significant ways (Seifer 1998).

- **Balance between service and learning objectives.** Clinical education emphasizes student learning as the primary objective, and service, if an objective at all, is secondary. Service-learning attempts to balance service and learning objectives. Medical schools and community partners must negotiate the differences in their needs and expectations when designing a service-learning course.

• **Emphasis on reciprocal learning.** In service-learning, the traditional definitions of "faculty," "teacher," and "learner" are intentionally blurred (Seifer, Mutha, and Connors 1996). Community members, agency staff, medical school faculty, and medical students can all serve in teaching and learning roles.

• **Emphasis on more than individual interactions.** Clinical education emphasizes student acquisition of clinical knowledge and skills, and focuses on the individual interactions between clinician and patient. Service-learning emphasizes the importance of addressing community-identified concerns, incorporating an understanding of broad factors influencing health and quality of life explicitly into the curriculum, and fostering citizenship skills.

• **Emphasis on reflective practice.** Clinical education emphasizes observing and doing, but does not typically emphasize or include opportunities for critical reflection. Reflection is a critical component of service-learning and facilitates the students' making connections between their service experiences and their learning (Eyler, Giles, and Schmiede 1996). Opportunities for critical reflection through dialogue, journals, stories, and other means encourage students to consider the larger social, political, economic, and cultural contexts of the community concerns being addressed through service-learning.

• **Integral role of community partners.** Even when clinical education takes place in community-based settings, the curriculum is most often designed by university-based faculty and delivered only in community-based settings. In service-learning, community partners are integrally involved in the design, implementation, and evaluation of the curriculum. Community partners are integral to designing service-learning experiences that are responsive to community concerns and priorities. For example, community groups commonly complain about having their needs assessed over and over again by students and faculty as part of student coursework and faculty research. Increasingly, service-learning courses are being designed that integrate students into ongoing community assessment and program development efforts, thus enabling them to contribute to and learn from these efforts without "re-creating the wheel" each semester. The integral role of community partners in service-learning can help prevent an exclusive focus on community *needs* by also considering those community *strengths* and *assets* that can be mobilized to build healthier communities (Kretzmann and McKnight 1993).

It is also important to distinguish service-learning from community service and volunteer activities. Service-learning is not required voluntarism.

Voluntarism is "the engagement of individuals in activities where the primary emphasis is in the service being provided and the primary intended beneficiary is clearly the service recipient" (Furco 1996: 4). Thus, voluntarism does not attempt to balance service and learning. Although medical student voluntarism should be encouraged and supported, the learning that occurs through volunteering is not structured and may be quite accidental. Without a reflective component, there may be no explicit connection made among the volunteer activity, the students' medical school coursework, and the students' future roles as physicians and citizens.

Purpose and Content of This Volume

This volume is intended to help the reader understand service-learning, how it differs from traditional clinical medical education, and how, as a form of experiential education, it can have a profound impact on students, faculty, communities, medical schools, and the relationships among these important stakeholders.

The volume begins by describing the broad context in which service-learning takes place, with O'Neil analyzing trends in the health-care system and Gardner et al. discussing the relevance of community-oriented primary care and continuous quality improvement to service-learning. Both predict a health-care system that will increasingly be centered around activities that take place outside the hospital setting, involve interdisciplinary teams of health professionals, and respond directly to the needs of communities. These delivery system changes are already having a profound impact on the process, content, and location of medical education, creating a fertile environment for service-learning.

Within this context, the next 10 chapters describe model programs and courses that embody different approaches to and respond to different challenges in integrating service-learning into the culture and curriculum of medical education. These models are drawn from both public and private universities in urban and rural settings, and include cocurricular as well as curricular programs, undergraduate as well as graduate medical education, clinical as well as nonclinical experiences. In highlighting these particular models, we are not suggesting that they represent the "right way" to integrate service-learning into medical education. Rather, they illustrate the diversity in organization, structure, goals, and methodology of service-learning, and provide examples of many ways to initiate and sustain service-learning in medical schools and residency programs. Particular attention is paid to the development and sustainability of community partnerships, upon which the effectiveness of all service-learning programs ultimately rests.

But despite the fact that the models described here demonstrate numerous approaches to integrating service-learning into medical education, they also show that there are specific principles and components that are critical to the success of any service-learning program.

The Community-Campus Partnership

As was just noted, a successful service-learning program necessarily involves a partnership that builds upon the capacities, resources, and needs of community participants, agency staff, medical students, participating faculty, and a medical institution. From the very beginning, partners need to articulate an explicit set of goals and expectations that all subscribe to. A mechanism to promote and allow for ongoing, open communication between community partners and school officials is another necessity. Finally, programs should, if possible, be linked to other community resources in order to more holistically approach the identified needs and to locate the students' service-learning experiences in a broader context. Community-Campus Partnerships for Health has advanced a set of principles of good community-campus partnerships that can help guide the development of effective service-learning partnerships (Community-Campus Partnerships for Health 1999):

1. Partners have agreed upon mission, values, goals, and measurable outcomes for the partnership.

2. The relationship between partners is characterized by mutual trust, respect, genuineness, and commitment.

3. The partnership builds upon identified strengths and assets, but also addresses areas that need improvement.

4. The partnership balances the power among partners and enables resources among partners to be shared.

5. There is clear, open, and accessible communication between partners, making it an ongoing priority to listen to each need, develop a common language, and validate/clarify the meaning of terms.

6. Roles, norms, and processes for the partnership are established with the input and agreement of all partners.

7. There is feedback to, among, and from all stakeholders in the partnership, with the goal of continuously improving the partnership and its outcomes.

8. Partners share the credit for the partnership's accomplishments.

9. Partnerships take time to develop and evolve over time.

Institutionalization

To promote short-term success and long-term sustainability, a service-learning program needs to be recognized as an integral part of the school that sponsors it, and the service that program provides as an important educational experience for physicians-in-training. Community partners, students, and faculty are more likely to get involved and stay committed if the institution formally acknowledges service-learning efforts as analogous to clinical work and coursework. Such acknowledgment is essential when recruiting faculty mentors, student leaders, and community preceptors, as there are few external rewards for assuming additional responsibilities.

Structure and Support

Service-learning is a pedagogy that fosters learning through both action and reflection. A program's structure and activities should therefore be designed to address this dual approach. First, students must be adequately prepared for their service work. Service-learning programs often involve students in new, challenging settings. Formal training is critical for students to develop the skills, knowledge, and understanding they will need to be useful partners in the community. Second, programs need to create opportunities for students to reflect on and explore the connections between their service and their classwork. This allows them to more thoroughly integrate and translate their community experiences into their medical training. Finally, it is beneficial to develop permanent systems that allow for ongoing and fluid leadership within service-learning programs. A central location where efforts can be coordinated and resources made available facilitates the efforts of students and community partners. An investment of time and institutional resources signals to all stakeholders the seriousness of the work and validates service-learning as a credible learning experience.

Assessment and Continuous Improvement

From a program's inception, a system for evaluating it should be in place, offering opportunities for all stakeholders to provide feedback on a regular basis in order to amend and grow the program as necessary.

Two more-general chapters conclude the volume. In the first, Tarallo-Falk examines the impact of service-learning on the socialization process that students typically go through during their medical education. In the second, Gelmon et al. report on early lessons learned from an external evaluation of the Health Professions Schools in Service to the Nation (HPSISN) program, a national demonstration program focusing on service-learning in health professions education. Both these chapters provide empirical support for service-learning's potential to prepare students for their roles as health professionals and citizens, change the way faculty teach, change the way health professions schools relate to their communities, enable community organizations and community members to play significant roles in how health professionals are educated, and enhance community capacity. The volume concludes with a description of recommended organizations, publications, and Web-based resources for integrating service-learning into medical education.

Service-learning is not only a strategy for preparing community-responsive and competent health physicians, it is also a strategy for fostering citizenship and changing the relationship between communities and medical schools. We hope this volume provides readers with a valuable source of information and inspiration to develop and expand service-learning across the continuum of medical education.

References

Barker, L.R. (1990). "Curriculum for Ambulatory Care Training in Medical Residency: Rationale, Attitudes, and Generic Proficiencies." *Journal of General Internal Medicine* 5(S): S3-S14.

Bellack, J. (1996). "Education for the Community." *Journal of Nursing Education* 34(8): 342-343.

Boelen, C. (1992). "Medical Education Reform: The Need for Global Action." *Academic Medicine* 67(11): 745-749.

Bok, D. (1982). *Beyond the Ivory Tower: Social Responsibilities of the Modern University.* Cambridge, MA: Harvard University Press.

Boyer, E.L. (1990). *Scholarship Reconsidered: Priorities of the Professoriate.* Princeton, NJ: Carnegie Foundation for the Advancement of Teaching.

Cohen, J.J. (1995). "Generalism in Medical Education: The Next Steps." *Academic Medicine* 70(1 Suppl): S7-S9.

Community-Campus Partnerships for Health. (1999). "Principles of Partnerships." San Francisco, CA: Community-Campus Partnerships for Health.

Council on Graduate Medical Education. (1995). *Report to Congress, 1995.* Washington, DC: Government Printing Office.

Desjardins, P. (1996). "Creating a Community-Oriented Curriculum and Culture: Lessons Learned From the 1993-1996 Ongoing New Jersey Experiment." *Journal of Dental Education* 60(10): 821-826.

Eyler, J., D. Giles, and A. Schmiede. (1996). *A Practitioner's Guide to Reflection in Service-Learning: Student Voices and Reflections.* Nashville, TN: Vanderbilt University Press.

Faller, H.S., et al. (1996). "Bridge to the Future: Nontraditional Clinical Settings, Concepts, and Issues." *Journal of Nursing Education* 34(8): 344-349.

Feltovich, J., et al. (1989). "Teaching Medical Students in Ambulatory Settings in Departments of Internal Medicine." *Academic Medicine* 64: 36-41.

Field, M.J., ed. (1995). *Dental Education at the Crossroads*. Washington, DC: National Academy Press.

Foreman, S. (1994). "Social Responsibility and the Academic Medical Center: Building Community-Based Systems for the Nation's Health." *Academic Medicine* 69(2): 97-102.

Furco, A. (1996). "Service-Learning: A Balanced Approach to Experiential Education." In *Expanding Boundaries: Serving and Learning*, edited by J. Raybuck, pp. 2-6. Washington, DC: Corporation for National Service.

Institute of Medicine, Committee for the Study of the Future of Public Health. (1988). *The Future of Public Health*. Washington, DC: National Academy Press.

Jacoby, B., ed. (1996). *Service-Learning in Higher Education: Concepts and Practices*. San Francisco, CA: Jossey-Bass.

Kolb, D.A. (1984). *Experiential Learning: Experience as a Source of Learning and Development*. Englewood Cliffs, NJ: Prentice-Hall.

Kretzmann, J., and J. McKnight. (1993). *Building Communities From the Inside Out*. Chicago, IL: ACTA Publications.

Lawrence, R.S. (1988). "The Goals for Medical Education in the Ambulatory Setting." *Journal of General Internal Medicine* 3(S): S5-S25.

Maurana, C.A., and K. Goldenberg. (1996). "A Successful Academic-Community Partnership to Improve the Public's Health." *Academic Medicine* 71(5): 425-431.

Pew Health Professions Commission. (1993). *Health Professions Education for the Future: Schools in Service to the Nation*. San Francisco, CA: Center for the Health Professions.

Sandoval, V.A. (1996). "President-Elect's Address, 1996 Annual Session: A View From the Crossroads." *Journal of Dental Education* 60(7): 550-552.

Schmidt, H.G., et al. (1991). "Network of Community-Oriented Educational Institutions for the Health Sciences." *Academic Medicine* 66: 259-263.

Seifer, S.D. (1998). "Service-Learning: Community-Campus Partnerships for Health Professions Education." *Academic Medicine* 73: 273-277.

Seifer, S.D., K. Connors, and E.H. O'Neil. (1996). "Combining Service and Learning in Partnership With Communities." *Academic Medicine* 71(5): 527.

Seifer, S.D., S. Mutha, and K. Connors. (1996). "Service-Learning in Health Professions Education: Barriers, Facilitators, and Strategies for Success." In *Expanding Boundaries: Serving and Learning*, edited by J. Raybuck, pp. 36-41. Washington, DC: Corporation for National Service

Smego, R.A., and J. Costante. (1996). "An Academic Health Center–Community Partnership: The Morgantown Health Right Free Clinic." *Academic Medicine* 71(6): 613-621.

Woolisscroft, J.O., and T.L. Schwenk. (1989). "Teaching and Learning in the Ambulatory Setting." *Academic Medicine* 64: 644-648.

The Changing Health-Care System and Expectations of Physicians

by Edward H. O'Neil

The transformation of health care is taking place at many levels. At the federal level, there are pieces of proposed legislation to radically reform the Medicare system. In more than one-half of the states, there are debates around the question of redefining the legitimate political interests of the states in the regulation and direction of health care. Some states propose additional regulation and some propose freer markets, but all are far more active in the discussion than ever before. At local levels, the reconfiguration of the health-care system goes on daily as employers move employees to capitated systems of care and as hospitals, insurance companies, and professional practice groups buy out one another in an effort to create new health-care organizations and systems.

As chaotic as all of this may seem, such developments are driven by an underlying logic. Since 1989, the Pew Health Professions Commission has been investigating this logic. The commission's first report, *Healthy America: Practitioners for 2005* (1989), assessed the forces that would likely impact the health-care system and all of its providers by the year 2005. These forces are characterized in Figure 1 as a set of tensions between what currently exists as the dominant paradigm in the health-care system and what will emerge over the next decade and a half. These trends are deliberately presented as tensions that seek a balance point between the left and right sides of Figure 1. Such tensions pervade health-care delivery and financing, the doctor-patient relationship, the provider-payer relationship, and the atmosphere within health professions educational institutions. They also provide the framework for examining and redefining the higher education mission of professional schools, federal and state relationships with health-care providers and delivery systems, health workforce planning, and public expectations for a changed health-care system. A shift in orientation or balance from left to right seems inevitable. It is in the interest of health professional groups, professional schools, delivery organizations, policymakers, and, ultimately, individual practitioners to understand these changes and make the necessary strategic accommodations. It is important to note that some professions, parts of professions, institutions, and practitioners will remain close in orientation to the current paradigm. The nation's health system will need such an orientation from these organizations and individuals, but it is important to realize how difficult and increasingly competitive it will become to maintain such an orientation.

Figure 1
Dynamic Tensions in Health Care

Current Paradigm	Emerging Paradigm
Specialized Care	Primary Care
Technologically Driven	Humanely Balanced
Cost Unaware	Cost Aware
Institutionally Based	Community Based
Governed Professionally	Governed Managerially
Acute Treatment	Chronic Management
Individual-Patient Focused	Population Perspective
Curative Care	Preventive Orientation
Individual Provider	Team Provider
Competition	Cooperation

Source: Pew Health Professions Commission 1989

To fully understand how these tensions drive reform, one must examine them more closely. The nation has experienced a 40-year period in which the health-care disciplines have grown increasingly specialized with the expansion of highly reductionist knowledge. Without a doubt, this trend has served many of the health needs of the public. However, there is growing recognition that this trend has also played a significant part in the rapid escalation of costs, the isolation of patients, and the lack of coordination of treatment. In the future, the nation will move to recapture a better balance between the generalist and the specialist, with the system increasingly turning to the generalist for direction and integration of care.

In part, this movement toward specialization of health care has occurred because of rapid growth in the availability of diagnostic and therapeutic technology. As these technologies have advanced, they have served the public, but they have also driven up costs and alienated patients from their own health. There is little doubt that Americans will continue to demand the latest in technology as it relates to their health and the health of their families, but they will increasingly recognize and value the balancing of technology with nontechnological approaches to health and wellness, such as health promotion and disease prevention. This demand for a combination of "high tech/high touch" will present a major opportunity to those professionals and delivery systems that can successfully integrate both. In terms of costs, those professionals and delivery systems that can demonstrate the effectiveness, efficiency, and cost savings of using particular technologies will be well positioned with payers and purchasers of care, who will continue to demand a high level of accountability.

At $1 trillion and 14 percent of the gross domestic product, there is little doubt that the cost of health care is a significant, if not the principal, driver of reform. The per capita expenditures for health care in the United States far exceed anything comparable in other industrialized countries. As the population ages and consumes more health care, there will be even greater pressure on costs. The single most important problem for health care as a whole over the next 20 years will be how to deliver more care of higher quality for fewer dollars. This crush for economic responsiveness will create a situation in which all the rules that have governed the care system will be reconsidered. Each profession and care-delivery organization will be forced to defend how it delivers care in the context of cost. This will require immediate attention to the collection of these data and long-term attention to development of the discipline needed to constantly design and implement ways to reduce cost and maintain or improve quality.

As health care grew over the past 50 years, it consistently moved into larger and larger institutions. Hospitals often are the largest employers in an area. Just as this trend has been a by-product of the specialization and growth of technology that has accompanied health care, so it will undoubt-edly be affected by other changes. Those parts of the health-care system that are accessible to the public and responsive to consumer demands, and can accommodate the patterns of contemporary life-styles will be the ones that are successful in the future. Many of the large institutions that have come to characterize the organization of health care will remain, but few will remain in their current configuration. To be successful in the future, they will of necessity add a larger ambulatory or community-based dimen-sion to their current operations, or they will develop partnerships with con-stituents of the health-care system that are now, or will soon emerge as, sig-nificantly established in the community.

The movement from a professionally dominated system of care, one in which health professionals control most decisions out of professional pre-rogatives, to one in which other, more managerially derived values come into consideration is a disturbing development to health professionals. It is one of the tensions most evident today. The past, in which health professionals were independent actors offering their services with little regulation by pub-lic or private parties, has for the most part vanished. The future will hold higher and higher standards of accountability enforced by a greater variety of regulating agencies in both the public and private sectors. The profes-sions, and to a lesser extent the institutions, of health care will resist this trend. It seems ultimately that this resistance will be in vain. The only way to be successful will be to fully understand the elements of the managerial paradigm and begin the process of incorporating them into basic profes-sional values and patterns of practice. Developing the skills and capacities to utilize outcomes data, develop practice guidelines, incorporate cost-effective strategies that do not compromise quality should be in the domain of values and skills for all health professionals. Professions and institutions that do this will be in a position to control more of their own destiny and still be responsive to the changing demands of the public.

The disease burden of the nation has shifted dramatically over the past 90 years. As we move through the next two decades, a similar shift will occur. For the first 40 years of the century, the nation focused on the treat-ment and the alleviation of acute disorders brought about by infectious agents. The contributions physicians could make were greatly increased by scientific advances and the corresponding development of new diagnostic and treatment technologies. With most life-threatening infectious disorders brought under control, for the past 50 years the attention of the medical community has been focused on the treatment of the acute manifestations of chronic disorders. The challenge for the future is to move to an approach that focuses on the prevention of disease and the management of chronic disease in a fashion that enhances quality of life. There will still be the need for trauma surgeons and restorative techniques in dentistry, but those professions or parts of professions and institutions that restrict themselves to these acute domains will do so at their own peril.

Closely related to this balance between the acute and chronic disability is the orientation of the health system. Clearly, the U.S. health-care system has been and remains very concerned with the treatment of individuals who have disease and disability. Such a focus is understandable and, in part, a necessary dimension of any health system. However, the reality of the demands of the health-care system of the future means that this orientation to treating or curing individuals needs to be balanced with one that prevents disease and disability in populations, and when increasingly chronic disabilities manifest themselves does a better job of managing patient needs and enhancing quality of life with available resources.

The complexities of the changing health-care system will demand a sophisticated response. The future will demand more generalists knowing more things in broad ways, rather than the focus on specialized knowledge that dominates health care today. However, the management of patients will grow increasingly complex as the population ages. To respond, successful professionals will broaden their identities as team members and providers. They will serve their patients and the public better as they develop skills of integration and draw upon a variety of colleagues both inside and outside the traditional health-care professions. Those professions most valued and revered will be those that can effectively integrate knowledge and professional skills over a number of different professional domains in order to develop services that respond to patient needs in an effective and timely manner. Ultimately, it will be the capacity to lead such teams that will be highly valued by the systems of care and the patients they serve.

Finally, the tension between competition and cooperation will play out as the health-care system redefines itself. Currently, there are legal, economic, and market forces that keep professionals, professional groups, and institutions from cooperating to create a better system of care. These impediments will disappear, and incentives will emerge to encourage more effective cooperation in the use of scarce health-care resources. Those institutions that early on develop the capacity to forge and sustain strategic partnerships will be well positioned to take advantage of the opportunities of a rapidly changing system. Those that do not risk being isolated without the diversity of resources to continue to make meaningful contributions to heath care.

Impact of the Tensions on Health-Care Reform

The tensions discussed here are obviously broad and certainly of debatable probability as health care moves toward the future. However, in many ways these tensions are already driving a significant level of reform within health care. The states, burdened with a spiraling Medicaid responsibility, are looking for any avenue that can help to bring them relief from financial obligation but still provide care for their citizens. Reforms at the state level include small business insurance reform, tort reform, waiver from Medicaid mandates in favor of experimental approaches, pressure to create more primary-care providers from state institutions, and efforts to broaden the practice acts to permit more care to be provided by a greater range of professionals. At the local or regional level, the health-care market seems unfazed by the demise of "accountable health plans" and "health alliances" as a part of federal legislation. Instead, physician groups, hospitals, and insurance companies are in a buying and selling frenzy to develop integrated service-delivery networks at the local level. These are bringing together primary-care networks, specialty and hospital care, and an insurance function that assumes financial risk and provides organization and systemization. These newly merged systems are also actively pursuing the development of systems to improve quality, lower cost, and improve patient satisfaction.

All of these changes must be factored in to examine and explore the impact of health-care reform on medical education. While public policies, funding authorities, program guidelines, new partners for collaboration, or market realities for all of these changes may not exist now or even in the near future, the general message as to how these trends will impact the educational, research, and patient-care dimensions of academic medical centers is increasingly clear. The policy changes at the federal, state, and market levels will produce a host of changes that will profoundly impact medical schools and teaching hospitals.

Impact of Reforms on Medical Education

There seem to be three issues of significance to medical education: first, the relative balance between the production of medical specialists and generalists; second, the size of the overall physician pipeline; and third, the relevance of the current medical curriculum to the practice challenges of generalist and specialist alike in a reconfigured delivery system.

The conclusion that the nation is producing too many medical specialists is without many dissenters. There are important exceptions in general surgery and psychiatry, but for the most part, most of the medical and surgical subspecialties and their equivalents in radiology, pathology, and anesthesiology are in oversupply given the demands of the current system. If one has projected an even modestly more capitated system of care by the year 2000, the supply of most subspecialists far exceeds any expectations of what will be needed. Less certain but potentially just as important is the seeming undersupply of primary-care physicians. Certainly, there will be no decrease in the number of training positions, but even if all available training positions were completely filled, it is not evident that there would be an increase in additional primary-care physician positions or whether these needs might be more appropriately and less expensively addressed by other primary-care providers.

For academic medical centers and medical schools, this means a dramatic decline in the number of specialty training positions available over the next five to 10 years. An adjustment will have to be made with some sort of rationing mechanism at the national level that will attempt to balance national and local needs, the need to maintain quality, service responsibilities of existing programs, and regional distribution. Nonetheless, if the oversupply is in the range of 25 to 50 percent, then regardless of location or quality, all graduate medical training programs will be affected. Furthermore, such a loss of positions will not be made up by gains in primary care. Hence, the impact of this change on the academic medical center could be significant. The available faculty will no longer match the training needs of the residents or institutions. Also, the service provided by residents will have to be provided by other physicians on staff or by other health professionals such as nurse practitioners, nurse clinical specialists, or physician assistants. There are significant economic implications in such a shift, because all of these professionals will cost more than residents to employ, they will work shorter hours, and their services may not be subsidized by the federal government.

The balance between specialists and generalists is only one part of the question of physician supply. There is a growing concern that the overall supply of physicians is too great for the current care-delivery arrangement and that in a reformed system the oversupply will be so large as to need policy attention. There is, of course, no direct federal policy mechanism for shrinking medical education, and the likelihood of concerted change from the state sector seems slight. However, if the projections by the Council on Graduate Medical Education have been accurate in anticipating an overall physician oversupply of 80,000 by the year 2000, then a reduction in the overall class size in medical education of up to 30 percent by 2005 is not out of the range of possibility.

Finally, the size and distribution of the physician population is in many ways less important to medical schools than is the task of educating physicians who have the skills to meet the demands of patient care. As the health-care system changes and the demands on the physician as health-care leader evolve, these skills will change. The Pew Health Professions Commission has pointed to a gap between what the future is likely to demand and what physicians feel confident in providing. Figure 2 identifies some of the emerging competencies for medical practice in the next century. Medical schools and residency programs will increasingly be held accountable for providing an education to meet these competencies — a challenging task, given the current medical education environment with its emphasis on the care of individual patients in specialized inpatient settings. To attain these competencies in their graduates, schools must examine the context and content of their curricula. As the subsequent chapters in this volume demonstrate, service-learning offers medical schools an approach and strategy for preparing their graduates for practice in the evolving health-care system.

Reference

Pew Health Professions Commission. (1989). *Healthy America: Practitioners for 2005.* Durham, NC: Pew Health Professions Commission.

Figure 2
Practitioner Competencies for 2005

- Care for the community's health
- Expand access to effective care
- Provide contemporary clinical care
- Emphasize primary care
- Participate in coordinated care
- Ensure cost-effective and appropriate care
- Practice prevention
- Involve patients and families in the decision-making process
- Promote healthy life-styles
- Assess and use technology appropriately
- Improve the health-care system
- Manage information
- Understand the role of the physical environment
- Provide counseling on ethical issues
- Accommodate expanded accountability
- Participate in a racially and culturally diverse society
- Continue to learn

Source: Pew Health Professions Commission 1989

Toward Building Communities of Commitment:
Integrating Community-Oriented Primary Care and Continuous Quality Improvement Into Service-Learning

by Deborah Gardner, Andrew Schamess, Doreen Harper, and Denice Cora-Bramble

It is 10 at night in a large, snow-covered city. In a top-story office, under fluorescent lights, an executive sifts through papers on his desk. He is responsible for managing a health-care company that owns several hospitals and nursing homes. He is evaluating a proposed marketing strategy designed to keep the company viable in the face of increased competition. Below, on the street, a homeless man settles onto the subway ventilation grating on the sidewalk where he usually sleeps. He is nearly blind from diabetes and has an infected skin ulcer on his left ankle. He has just left the emergency room of a nearby hospital. As he pulls an old wool blanket over his head, a nurse sits in a cubicle finishing his discharge papers. She sees that this was his eighth emergency room visit this year and that he has no other source of primary care. What, she wonders, will become of him? Momentarily, she questions her own professional integrity. Could she have done more for this patient?

The characters described above occupy niches within a complicated health-care structure. Each acts to maintain equilibrium in the particular fragment of the system he or she controls. Living in apparently separate worlds and engaged in tasks they do not perceive as interconnected, they are unlikely to ever meet to share ideas or devise solutions, but the unique knowledge each one carries of the problems in the system, if harnessed, would represent a powerful force for constructive change.

This scenario illustrates some of the unintended outcomes of the U.S. health-care system. We can direct extraordinary intellectual and technical resources toward the medical care of some patients, but others are denied basic care. Despite vast expenditures and huge profits in the health-care field, the United States still has excessively high rates of infant death and preventable disease among low-income and ethnic minority groups (Gornick et al. 1996; Singh and Yu 1996; Smith et al. 1996a, 1996b; Sorlie, Backlund, and Keller 1995; Wright 1993). Health insurance plans vie for wealthy subscribers, while morbidity and mortality rates in some segments of the population rival those in developing countries (Friedman et al. 1996; Kassirer 1996). The groups most affected are those that have the least access to society's wealth and are the most vulnerable to illness (Kaplan et al. 1996; Kennedy, Kawachi, and Prothrow-Smith 1996; Semanza et al. 1996). As the redistribution of health-care resources proceeds, driven more by market forces than by humanitarian goals, there is growing concern that inequities will become even greater and opportunities fewer for low-income and ethnic minority groups (Schroeder 1996; Smith et al. 1996a, 1996b).

Despite current trends, we believe that the potential exists as it always has for a health-care system that is rational, humane, and driven by the needs of communities. Such a system will come about not by governmental fiat but through individuals who perceive the need for change and are willing to establish and work toward common goals at the local level. Service-learning has been advanced as an educational model that can help to instill in health professionals the motivation and skills to undertake this work (Seifer, Sunita, and Conners 1996). Service-learning extends the classroom into the community, and thus creates a physical space that brings together people with differing social, ethnic, and professional backgrounds, and with correspondingly diverse perspectives.

Placement alone, however, is not sufficient to bring about lasting change in individuals or in communities. Sponsorship of student activities must be accompanied by constructive action on the part of educational institutions in the area of community health. Education for change — humanizing health professional education — occurs in the context of praxis. Productive collaboration between universities and other segments of the community requires the development of a conceptual forum: a set of mutually understood ideas and a common language so that dialogue can take place. Goodwin Liu (1995) reminds us that a community — even one in crisis — will not relinquish an old paradigm until a new one has been *fully* developed and challenges all to be honest about the unfinished work in this field. Constructs embedded in separate disciplines can and must be merged in order to establish a basis for collective learning and subsequent action to improve health care.

In pursuit of this common language, we propose systems theory as a bridging paradigm for exploring the connections between "community-oriented primary care" (COPC) as developed by Sidney Kark and his followers (Nutting and Garr 1989) and "systemic continuous quality improvement" (SCQI) as described by Daniel Kim (1990) and Paul Batalden (Batalden, Nelson, and Roberts 1994). These can be viewed as two mental models, based in different disciplines, each geared toward health-care improvement. Their integration provides a potential basis from which to work toward sustainable, inclusive community-based health care, thus creating a template for broader, collaborative service-learning initiatives.

This integrative process itself also serves as an example of the sort of cross-disciplinary discussion that should form the substrate of service-learning. Following thinkers such as Walter Ong (1979) and Paulo Freire (1995), we view education not as a didactic monologue directed from teacher to student, covering preexisting curricular material, but instead as a dialogic process engaging all those who have a stake in community health, a process in which all parties both teach and learn. For service-learning to be effective, this dialogue must take place simultaneously in the academic setting and at the interface of academy and community. Faculty must be prepared to listen, to facilitate, and to empower learners to act on their vision. If true dialogue is allowed to spread within and beyond the academic institution, it has the power to unleash the knowledge and energy that exist throughout communities as a force for constructive change in a way that a more exclusionary planning process never could.

The wide range of perspectives involved here calls for a model that can encompass a multitude of potential strategies, while remaining grounded in a shared ethical vision for the health professions. In this article, we propose that systems thinking as described by Senge (1990) be adopted as an essential component of service-learning. Systems thinking offers a way of managing the interconnections between various functions in the context of health policy and planning, as well as in the context of developing a service-learning curriculum. It increases our ability to perceive problems on the basis of the whole, rather than breaking them into parts. It therefore provides a framework for the integration of the different perspectives inherent in the dialogic process, and a viable alternative to the narrow discipline-bound nature of much current education and practice.

COPC and CQI: Identifying Common Ground

As the tension between health care as a professional service and as a business has heightened, COPC and CQI have become divergent reference points. COPC evolved as an ecological model integrating the disciplines of medicine and public health, and focusing on community health issues. CQI is based on involving all workers in identifying problems and improving products or service, and originates in business management (Kim 1990). Often, COPC and CQI have been taught from a utilitarian viewpoint, without connection to their original systemic philosophies. As methods, they have been effective in very different contexts (public health and business, respectively), which tends to make them appear incompatible. In the current, competitive environment, the perceived dominance of one technique over another can evoke strong disciplinary loyalties in students and faculty, and undermine efforts to develop interdisciplinary experiences.

The excessive valuation of technique in health-care education (operational learning) undermines deeper reflection, but the *why* or conceptual learning that challenges the assumptions behind applied practice can serve to reframe problems in new and creative ways. While their origins and methods differ, COPC and CQI are both philosophies and techniques for planning change based on data-driven problem solving. The philosophical underpinnings of COPC and CQI are holistic in nature and complement the service-learning foundation. Before using COPC and CQI to derive a structure for service-learning, we will present a conceptual overview of each approach.

Community-Oriented Primary Care (COPC)

The concept of community-oriented primary care evolved in the 1960s and 1970s, partly in response to the fragmentation that accompanied the rapid growth of technology and specialization of medical care. Sidney Kark observed that "in more developed countries, health and welfare services are often provided by separate agencies having little, if any, accountability to one another, to a central authority, or to the community itself" (Kark and Abramson 1982: 122). In contrast, the COPC-directed health-care provider was to accept "responsibility for care of all the people, not only those with particular medical needs that require the facilities for tertiary care" (122).

Kark envisioned COPC less as a standardized method for community health improvement than as a complex, mutualistic interplay between clinician and community, in that the "numerator" (the individual patient) was inextricably connected to the "denominator" (the population with its patterns of disease). A student described his early experiences in Kark's practice in South Africa as follows: "The walls of the examining, consulting, and conference rooms at Polela and Lamontville were lined with charts and graphs of community demography, infant mortality rates, and their change over time. It was almost impossible not to be aware of denominators when seeing an individual patient" (Geiger 1982: 124). Thus, the provider is able to move comfortably between caring for the individual and the community. Community input and participation in both clinical and outreach initiatives is a key feature of COPC (Robinson 1982; Taylor 1990).

A number of successful COPC demonstration projects have been reported, some of which have accumulated several decades of experience (Institute of Medicine 1982). Such projects have received extensive support from governments and foundations. In the United States, however, despite its conceptual appeal, COPC has been difficult to put into practice on a wide scale. It has certainly not emerged as a viable model for small community-based practices, the setting in which it was first envisioned. O'Connor (1989) has pointed out that COPC seems to work best when all the necessary services for a given population are centrally planned and funded, as is the case of government- and foundation-supported demonstration projects. In contrast, "in the pluralistic, fee-for-service U.S. health-care system, the defined communities that are at the heart of COPC are very difficult to bring into focus" (206). Ironically, the "competitiveness, diversity, and lack of coordination" that, according to O'Connor, "make application of COPC a practical impossibility for most practicing physicians" are the exact features that were identified as inefficiencies by Kark and for which COPC was proposed as a solution (208).

In an attempt to defend COPC as a practicable model, one group of advocates has recommended that the definition of "a community" be loosened to include any patients under the care of a particular organization or practitioner (Calvert 1990; Garr 1982). According to Nutting and Garr (1989), "The critical factor is to identify a population (denominator) and accept responsibility for offering health services relevant to the needs and demands of the identified population" (4). This allows central planning of services for at least a subgroup of the community. However, the social, anthropological, and historical features of communities that serve to enhance the understanding between practitioner and patient and invigorate the COPC practice do not apply to subscriber lists and other arbitrary groupings. Furthermore, dividing the community conceptually in such a way as to accept responsibility only for those who can and do subscribe to a particular health plan accentuates the fragmentation of care in existing geographic communities, and creates pools of high-risk indigent patients who are excluded altogether from the system.

It seems likely that, for the foreseeable future in the United States, the responsibility for providing health-care services to the residents of a given geographic area will remain divided among a multitude of public and private entities, ranging from individual practitioners to large hospital chains and public health bureaucracies. For as long as this is the case, we believe an approach to COPC that requires centralized planning and service provision will not be feasible on a large scale.

An alternative approach, which has not been extensively discussed in the COPC literature, would be one of decentralized care that is nonetheless cooperative and coordinated. In this model, the practitioner who wishes to pursue Kark's goal of providing "care for all of the people" in a community directs his or her energy not just toward an internal rearrangement of his or her own practice but also toward collaboration with other health-care providers (Kark and Abramson 1982). Patients and representatives of the various members of the community, including private business and government, need to be included in planning at this level. In addition to epidemiologic information, data must be gathered on health-care utilization and costs, and business and marketing strategies. Participants must believe, or be convinced, that their financial, social, and organizational goals will be better served, at least in some areas, by collaboration than by competition or mutual disregard. Any initiatives to restructure health care that are generated by this process will of necessity be based on a plurality of ideas and interests rather than on any one vision or theory. However, community-wide coalitions have effectively addressed important population health problems and at present offer the most effective model for large-scale, coordinated community-directed health initiatives (Cronin 1994; Rodat, Bader, and Veatch 1994).

Managing such a process requires as much skill in administration as in public health or medicine. It is at this point that the complementary qualities of COPC and CQI become evident. Both are derived from an attempt to look at systems holistically, to identify problems using objective data, and to improve institutions by incorporating multiple perspectives. COPC contains the knowledge necessary to perceive disease organically in a community, with its roots in social dysfunction and its manifestation in individuals, and to alter disease patterns to improve community health. However, the tools for creating a shared vision, analyzing organizational processes, and identifying leverage points for change — the tools necessary to build and maintain the collaborative structures that can accomplish COPC goals — are better developed in the field of CQI. Although CQI remains focused on intrainstitutional change, many of its methods are adaptable to interorganizational collaborative processes (Kalzuny 1995).

Continuous Quality Improvement (CQI)

CQI has proved, in many sectors of the economy including the health field, to be a powerful tool for evaluating and improving the quality of products and services. Deming (1981) and Juran (Juran and Gryna 1988) are credited with the initial formulation of this concept, which called for reframing the idea of separating cost and quality, understanding it as a dynamic tension rather than as an either/or decision. The need for closer worker involvement in the process of developing quality and the need for management to recognize the organizational system as a part of both the problem and the answer represent two ideas that have been especially influential in CQI's development.

Operationally, CQI began with an emphasis on *products,* on inspecting-out defects, but became extended to quality in *design* from the very beginning. Inclusion of the product development process created the need to include the entire company in quality control activities. Quality improvement was no longer an isolated function but an organization-wide activity. It is indisputable that the application of CQI tools to product and service organizations has been highly successful (Kim 1990).

The application of CQI to health care, as a service industry, has increased within the managed-care environment. When service is the product, customer retention becomes the quality focus. Service, however, is much more complicated than a product, especially when health care is the context. Offering quality care requires health professionals and administrators to develop a "common meaning" for their work and an ability to develop an understanding of different perspectives.

Outcomes of care as described by Donabedian introduced the quality trilogy, a framework to evaluate structure, processes, and outcomes as inseparable parts of the whole health-care system. The Serial "V" method developed by Batalden and associates (1994) rests upon the progressive linking of process knowledge through evaluation of improvement cycles connected to identified goals and outcomes. These are two well-known CQI models that have been effectively adapted into the health-care context.

The CQI emphasis on the involvement of all employees for quality improvement has often resulted in greater collaborative efforts across departments and increased the value of interdisciplinary efforts to reach common goals that could not be reached separately. Facilitated meetings that respectfully explore different perspectives create a broader understanding of many complex problems. Larger organizational goals are held in tension as departmental actions are developed for more effective alignment. The seven basic tools of CQI (Pareto chart, cause-and-effect diagram, check sheet, histogram, scatter diagram, stratification, and control charts) are relatively easy to understand, with well-defined guidelines for the use of each tool. The CQI philosophy has increased health-care management's recognition of the importance of clinical input and commitment in planning and implementing effective organizational change. Reciprocally, health-care clinicians have increasingly been able to understand that the ability to improve patient care lies *both* in the delivery of care *and* in participating in organizational forums focused on using different perspectives to improve the structures that deliver care.

CQI is an effective philosophy of the whole enterprise and a set of tools applicable at all levels of an organization. It is a *blend* of the micro and macro; it is the combination of a business management philosophy and the tools that makes it a powerful discipline. Without the tools, CQI is a guiding idea without a means to implement it. Using the tools alone, applied to problems only as they arise, creates a reactive environment (Kim 1990). This can also lead to an analysis of problems that fails to synthesize implications, thus optimizing components of a system rather than the "whole" of the system. Rooted in the commercial world, CQI has been primarily implemented at the intraorganizational level. Its fragmented use or misuse, serving to reduce costs in the short run but also to compromise quality, has led to its being perceived negatively by many health-care professionals.

Fragmented Practice Versus Systems Theory

Approaching CQI and COPC simply as techniques for outcome and process improvement brings out superficial similarities between the two methods. One needs only to specify health improvement as the desired outcome and designate a target population (such as a health plan's subscribers), and the CQI process can be followed to improve the health of this population — in evident fulfillment of the basic goals of COPC. However, this common approach, focused exclusively on technique, obscures the actual or unintended consequences of strategies for health-care delivery upon "whole" communities. For example, a CQI initiative that reduces the length of stay after childbirth at a given hospital, but does not concern itself with improving access to prenatal care in areas with high infant mortality, is neglecting a more crucial problem in the community as a whole. From a systems perspective, limited interventions result in unplanned negative outcomes — in this case, private hospitals' providing prenatal care to the poor in emergency rooms, heavy demand for expensive neonatal intensive care, increased infant mortality rates, and reduced human capital and lower quality of life in the community. In the social as in the individual body, chronic illness worsens when interventions that simply reduce symptoms are implemented.

In *The Fifth Discipline: The Art and Practice of the Learning Organization* (1990) as well as elsewhere, Senge challenges the dominant professional paradigm of specialization and positivistic/hypothetical deductive reasoning as having limited effectiveness in understanding many of today's complex problems. Our tendency to focus on external dramatic events can be counterproductive in a world of gradually emerging systemic crises. He offers the ideas that today's problems are a result of our past solutions and that many primary threats are slow, gradual processes — environmental pollution, chronic illnesses, the decay of the community and family structures.

Systems theory is not new, but its application to community, organization, team, and individual learning processes, as described by Senge, provides an integrated perspective for understanding problems and integrating actions. He describes the necessity of developing learning organizations, i.e., organizations that will succeed because they can adapt rapidly to a turbulent environment through openness to uncertainty and a continuous willingness to learn. He asserts that deep learning is not about figuring out the truth but about developing new capacities for effective action. By challenging our most basic assumptions, systems theory allows new learning to occur. However, organizational learning requires mutual participation — cooperative learning for coordinated action. Conversation becomes generative, looking for the causes of the symptom by viewing a problem from multiple levels. In a complex situation, using analysis alone will not produce an understanding of the system. It is the integration, the synthesis of perspectives, that creates new understandings.

Kofman and Senge (1993) propose the development of collaborative processes through the application of systems theory to cooperative problem solving. The underlying assumptions of this framework include these:

1. Systems thinking requires understanding the primacy of interdependency (inductive reasoning must be as well developed by professionals as deductive reasoning).

2. Complex problems require multiple perspectives if they are to be understood; thus, collaboration and dialogic inquiry in teams are essential.

3. Identified shared values can create commitment and change the context for exploring differences.

The fundamental principle of systems dynamics is that the structure of a dynamic system determines the behavior of individuals within that system. From this point of view, fundamental change occurs only if the structure itself is affected. One example would be the development of interdisciplinary collaborative experiences early in the socialization of students in the health-care professions. Under the right circumstances, this structural change could lead to a new mode of professional education that emphasizes the complementarity between shared goals and individual professional competence. However, for this to occur, the initial collaborative ideals must be allowed to foster generative dialogue across disciplinary and institutional boundaries, and, most important, the institution must be flexible enough to accept and implement the solutions that grow out of this dialogue. Structured interdisciplinary experiences will not change the long-term attitudes of students toward collaboration unless the energy generated by collaboration can be turned to transformative work.

It is evident from this that faculty developing interdisciplinary curricula must complement these efforts with effective collaborative structures at other levels inside and outside their institution. The development of a shared mental model integrating COPC and CQI is an example of a structural change at one level. Developing shared mental models improves our ability to communicate conceptually across disciplines and organizations. Currently, much of health-care professionals' training consists of taking in information. Learning is also about understanding how we think and challenging our most basic assumptions.

Systems thinking is a conceptual model for understanding interdependent and dynamic systems. A second important systems principle is that symptoms are different from causes and usually appear at a place and time removed from their source. An example of this is the currently high level of expenditures in health care on disease treatment, with little attention paid to prevention, and increasing neglect of those at highest risk of disease. In our health system, we have come to rely on interventions that ameliorate symptoms and leave causes unaffected (Senge and Asay 1989).

Paradoxically, systems thinking at the level of the individual organism is well developed in the medical sciences. Plausible models exist connecting organic insult to tissue pathology and disease symptoms through complex chains of interconnected biological events occurring over long periods of time. This approach has led to great therapeutic advances based on treatment, where possible, of etiology rather than of symptomatology. However, disciplinary boundaries have prevented health professionals from applying the same approach at the social level. Increasingly, mortality patterns worldwide and in the United States have come to be determined more by population access to appropriate care than by the existence of therapeutic options (Sorlie, Backlund, and Keller 1995). Indeed, if the challenges of medicine in this century were therapeutic, those in the next will be distributional. Preparation of health-care professionals for these challenges will require a firm grounding in the social application of systems theory to health care.

A New Synthesis

As noted earlier, for service-learning to be lasting and significant, it must be advanced at conceptual and operational learning levels. Systems thinking bridges COPC and CQI as complementary orientations that synergistically build a shared understanding of community issues and strategies.

Systemically, COPC and CQI are structurally organized to improve service processes and outcomes. The COPC model originally focused on the individual practitioner caring for the community. As teams of providers deliver care, CQI methods provide processes to coordinate action. Even more important, as it is recognized that the care provision is spread across many institutions and locations, CQI provides a prototype for systemic interinstitutional collaboration to respond to quantitative and qualitative health data. Systemic CQI promotes the value of interdisciplinary collaboration and provides methods to guide teams as complementary units for learning and leading change. Systemic CQI can integrate both "hard" and "soft" data for problem formulation with emphasis on both the analysis and the synthesis of problems. Senge (1990) and Kim (1990) offer dynamic systems-thinking tools to complement existing CQI tools.

COPC provides the organic vision of the community and the fundamental ethic of service to drive community health improvement. Both COPC and

CQI involve recipients in the planning of services. As COPC is rooted in a community perspective, CQI has been organization-focused. However, systemic CQI would reframe organizational actions as interdependent within the larger community system. Recently, in fact, CQI has been effectively applied to the community (Borland, Smith, and Nankivil 1994; Jackson et al. 1994; Pittman 1994). However, the transition from intra- to interorganizational activities represents a quantum leap in organizational complexity — from the organization to the community (Kalzuny 1995). Creativity in successfully working with the tension between organization and community needs will require community leaders to share information collaboratively and to develop trusting relationships that are cooperative rather than competitive. Equally important is a commitment to the values of learning from different perspectives. Systemically integrated, COPC and CQI afford a way to construct public, testable ways for reaching community health outcomes and for advancing service-learning. Differences or inherent strengths of the two constructs are summarized in the table that follows on the next page.

Operationalizing a Service-Learning Model

Developing a socially integrated, population-centered problem-solving model that can serve to enhance a service-learning commitment is the challenge. Through the service-learning vision of unifying professional development with meeting public need, students can use systems thinking to integrate conceptually current community health-care models and actual community experiences. To be sure, there exists a risk in using multiple models. The use of too many terms can overwhelm learners and make for muddied understanding rather than a broader perspective. Furthermore, every effort to clarify is at the same time concealing. However, since we cannot hold all possible perspectives at once, we have to choose among and then integrate operational models in order to further develop service-learning. These models must be flexible to reflect a dynamically changing context and integrate new ideas that emerge, yet stable enough to keep the shared goals of service-learning visible in actions and outcomes.

Up until now, there has been incremental change in the integration of COPC and CQI, with respectful attention being paid to each faculty member's primary orientation. CQI processes have been used to develop a shared vision, operational plans, and an evaluation mechanism in the course of organizing interdisciplinary faculty collaboration within and across organizational boundaries. CQI meeting tools have been used to guide the *process* of discussions about data collected from COPC methods in student teams. Community and university faculty partners identify either COPC or CQI as

Differences/Strengths: Community-Oriented Primary Care (COPC) Versus Systemic Continuous Quality Improvement (SCQI)

COPC	SCQI
• Strong value of understanding the needs of the whole community	• Vision of organization as part of a larger community
• Community-based tools for grass-roots organizations and outreach — epidemiology feedback loop	• Strong methods — organizationally based tools for team collaboration, synthesis and analysis of issues — PDSA (plan, do, study, act) cycles as feedback loops
• Emphasis on population health as the essential outcome	• Emphasis on the interdependence of all participants in service delivery and interdependence with the community
• Individual health status closely related to economic and social circumstances	• Values include shared learning and accountability
• Values include civic responsibility and community improvement	• Outcomes-focused

a primary framework for community project development and, through inquiry, have explored the concepts and methodology from the two approaches. Faculty are slowly acknowledging their learning from each other — an openness to the validity of different yet complementary perspectives. Recognition of the faculty expertise within these two models has led to increased project commitment by all. Communication of ideas has increased across disciplines and organizations as systems thinking has led to a greater recognition of the interdependence of all and the unique perspective of each. As projects reach completion, evaluation of the effectiveness of COPC and CQI concepts and methods in achieving project outcomes will give new understanding and direction to the continued use and interdependence of these two frameworks.

From a community perspective, it remains to be seen whether the dialogue occurring at the faculty level, the experiences of students in urban service-learning sites, and the necessary knowledge that resides in the community can be successfully integrated. A great deal of learning, both concrete and abstract, has occurred among all participants. There has been active collaboration between university- and community-based personnel in the areas of teaching and patient care. However, a huge disproportion in power and resources still separates the community sites from their university partners — a disproportion that poses its greatest challenge to the students who move back and forth between the two worlds and try to reconcile them. These students carry within themselves the rudiments of a true transformational dialogue. But the ability of faculty to elicit different perspectives, to recognize where the universities and the community sites fit in the larger systemic picture, and to facilitate action and support structural change will ultimately determine the integrity of the students' experiences. We hope that the synthesis of ideas presented in this article will contribute to creating a common intellectual ground, and a practical strategy, for pursuing the complementary goals of service-learning education and community health improvement.

Conclusion

Upon graduating, health-care students — like the nurse, the executive, and the homeless man in the opening scenario — will all find themselves enmeshed in a system that determines and constrains their options for community involvement. If health-care professionals are to reach out effectively to other professionals and redirect care toward community needs, then the professional socialization of all health-care professionals must include an understanding of the overall system and development of the skills necessary for intra- and interorganizational change. Effective service-learning will challenge learners to examine the relationship between ideas and action. They will begin to grasp their place and responsibility in the larger system that constitutes health care in this country. They will extend their attention beyond the requirements of a particular position or institution to the needs of communities.

In this article, we have outlined a conceptual basis for improving health care and creating a context for service-learning. COPC and CQI, holistically applied, provide a conceptual framework as well as many of the tools needed to strengthen the foundation of service-learning. However, it is not sufficient for faculty simply to assimilate theory and transmit it to students. We are all participants in a health-care system marked by widening disparities in health-care access, with no centralized mechanism for the equitable distribution of resources. In such an environment, activism needs to accompany teaching. Community members and university-based faculty must continue to work together to create a health-care system that is more just and efficient. This requires extensive cross-institutional collaboration, some sharing of power and resources, and a commitment to genuine change within ourselves.

References

Batalden, P.B., E.C. Nelson, and J.S. Roberts. (April 1994). "Linking Outcomes Measurement to Continual Improvement: The Serial "V" Way of Thinking About Improving Clinical Care." *Journal of Quality Improvement* 20(4): 167-178.

Borland, M., C. Smith, and N. Nankivil. (1994). "A Community Quality Initiative for Health Care Reform." *Managed Care Quarterly* 2: 6-16.

Calvert, J.F. (1990). "The Use of Community-Oriented Primary Care Techniques in Health Maintenance Organizations." In *Community-Oriented Primary Care,* edited by P. Nutting. Cambridge, MA: MIT, Sloan School of Management.

Cronin, C. (1994). "Business Coalitions on Health: Their Activities and Impact." *The Joint Commission Journal on Quality Improvement* 20: 376-379.

Deming, E.W. (1981). *Out of the Crisis.* Cambridge, MA: MIT.

Freire, P. (1995). *Pedagogy of the Oppressed.* New York, NY: Continuum.

Friedman, L.N., M.T. Williams, T.P. Singh, et al. (1996). "Tuberculosis, AIDS, and Death Among Substance Abusers on Welfare in New York City." *New England Journal of Medicine* 334: 828-833.

Garr, D.G. (1990). "COPC as a Marketing Strategy." In *Community-Oriented Primary Care,* edited by P. Nutting. Cambridge, MA: MIT, Sloan School of Management.

Geiger, H.J. (1982). "The Meaning of Community-Oriented Primary Care in an American Context." In *Institute of Medicine Conference Proceedings: Community-Oriented Primary Care,* edited by F. Mullan and C. Conner, pp. 120-133. Washington, DC: National Academy Press.

Gornick, M., P. Eggers, T.W. Reilly, et al. (1996). "Effects of Race and Income on Mortality and Use of Services Among Medicare Beneficiaries." *New England Journal of Medicine* 335: 791-799.

Institute of Medicine. (1982). *Conference Proceedings: Community-Oriented Primary Care. Part II, Practical Applications.* Washington, DC: National Academy Press.

Jackson, R.S., L.S. Leininger, R.P. Harris, et al. (1994). "Implementing Continuous Quality Improvement in Primary Care: Implications for Preventive Services." *Journal of Ambulatory Care Management* 17: 8-14.

Juran, J.M., and F.M. Gryna, eds. (1988). *Juran's Quality Control Handbook.* 4th ed. New York, NY: McGraw-Hill.

Kalzuny, A.D. (1995). "Quality Improvement: Beyond the Institution." *Hospital and Health Service Administration* 40(1): 172-188.

Kaplan, G.A., E.R. Pamuk, J.W. Lynch, et al. (1996). "Inequality in Income and Mortality in the United States: Analysis of Mortality and Potential Pathways." *British Medical Journal* 312: 999-1003.

Kark, S.L., and J.H. Abramson. (1982). "Community-Oriented Primary Care: Meaning and Scope." In *Institute of Medicine Conference Proceedings: Community-Oriented Primary Care,* edited by F. Mullan and C. Conner, pp. 134-150. Washington, DC: National Academy Press.

Kassirer, J.P. (1996). "The New Health Care Game." *New England Journal of Medicine* 335: 433.

Kennedy, B.P., I. Kawachi, and D. Prothrow-Smith. (1996). "Income Distribution and Mortality: Cross-Sectional Ecological Study of the Robin-Hood Index in the United States." *British Medical Journal* 312: 1004-1007.

Kim, D. (1990). *Toward Learning Organizations: Integrating Total Quality Management and Systems Thinking.* Cambridge, MA: MIT, Sloan School of Management.

Kofman, F., and P. Senge. (Autumn 1993). "Communities of Commitment: The Heart of Learning Organizations." *Organizational Dynamics* 22(2).

Liu, G. (January 1995). "Service-Learning: A Paradigm Change in Higher Education." Speech delivered at the Colloquium on National and Community Service sponsored by the American Association for Higher Education and Campus Compact, Washington, DC.

Nutting, P.A., and D.R. Garr. (September 1989). "Community-Oriented Primary Care." Monograph No. 124. Home Study Self-Assessment Program. Kansas City, MO: American Academy of Family Physicians.

O'Connor, P.J. (1989). "Is Community-Oriented Primary Care a Viable Concept in Actual Practice? An Opposing View." *Journal of Family Practice* 28(2): 206-208.

Ong, W. (1979). *Ramus, Method, and the Decay of Dialogue*. New York, NY: Octagon.

Pittman, M. (1994). "Measuring and Improving Community Health." *The Quality Letter for Healthcare Leaders* 6(5): 2-22.

Robinson, C. (1982). "Community Involvement in COPC." In *Community-Oriented Primary Care,* edited by P. Nutting. Cambridge, MA: MIT, Sloan School of Management.

Rodat, C.C., B.S. Bader, and R. Veatch. (1994). "Measuring and Improving Community Health." *The Quality Letter for Healthcare Leaders* 6: 2-21.

Schroeder, S.A. (1996). "The Medically Uninsured: Will They Always Be With Us?" *New England Journal of Medicine* 334: 1130-1133.

Seifer, S.D., S. Mutha, and K. Conners. (1996). "Service-Learning in Health Professions Education: Barriers, Facilitators, and Strategies for Success." In *Expanding Boundaries: Service and Learning,* edited by J. Raybuck, pp. 36-41. Washington, DC: Corporation for National Service.

Semanza, J.C., C.H. Rubin, K.H. Falter, et al. (1996). "Heat-Related Deaths During the July 1995 Heat Wave in Chicago." *New England Journal of Medicine* 335: 84-90.

Senge, P. (1990). *The Fifth Discipline: The Art and Practice of the Learning Organization*. New York, NY: Doubleday.

———— , and D. Asay. (May/June 1989). "Rethinking the Healthcare System." *Healthcare Forum Journal*, pp. 32-34+.

Singh, G.K., and S.M. Yu. (1996). "U.S. Childhood Mortality, 1950 Through 1993: Trends and Socioeconomic Differentials." *American Journal of Public Health* 86: 505-512.

Smith, G.D., J.D. Neaton, D. Wentworth, et al. (1996a). "Socioeconomic Differentials in Mortality Among Men Screened for the Multiple Risk Factor Intervention Trial: I. White Men." *American Journal of Public Health* 86: 486-496.

———— . (1996b). "Socioeconomic Differentials in Mortality Among Men Screened for the Multiple Risk Factor Intervention Trial: II. Black Men." *American Journal of Public Health* 86: 497-504.

Sorlie, P.D., E. Backlund, and J.B. Keller. (1995). "U.S. Mortality by Economic, Demographic, and Social Characteristics: The National Longitudinal Mortality Study." *American Journal of Public Health* 85: 949-956.

Taylor, H. (1990). "Use of a Cooperative Board Structure to Enhance Community Support." In *Community-Oriented Primary Care,* edited by P. Nutting. Albuquerque, NM: University of New Mexico Press.

Wright, R.A. (1993). "Community-Oriented Primary Care: The Cornerstone of Health-Care Reform." *Journal of the American Medical Association* 269(19): 2544-2547.

Partners in Health Education:
Service-Learning by First-Year Medical Students

by Joseph F. Walsh, Jennifer Sage Smith, G. Christian Jernstedt,
Virginia A. Reed, and Sara Goodman

First-year students at Dartmouth Medical School may elect to teach health at K-8 schools in the Dartmouth and Upper Connecticut River Valley region through the Partners in Health Education course. This elective is offered twice each year, during the fall and winter terms of the medical school Year One curriculum. Students teach a minimum of five lessons to a single class of children in a public elementary school and participate in three seminars that feature teaching and classroom management techniques, peer collaboration, and structured reflection. Organizational and wrap-up sessions complete the elective experience. Students may teach individually or in teams of two. Credit is awarded for successful completion of the course's activities.

Course Goals and Objectives

The Partners elective supports Year One medical students in their efforts to:
  • develop and refine skills of presenting health information to children;
  • provide quality health education lessons to children in area schools;
  • frame basic science content in clinically relevant prevention messages;
  • establish ties to communities in which they live and work, including ties to nonmedical professionals in those communities;
  • understand and celebrate the excitement of serving people as medical/health professionals.
By the end of the course, students are expected to have developed:
  • an understanding of and appreciation for the developmental level of children in primary, elementary, and middle school grades — with concentrated knowledge in one age range;
  • skill in identifying developmentally appropriate health messages and teaching methods;
  • skill in creating and implementing a lesson plan;
  • skill in communicating the core message in a presentation;
  • appreciation of the role medical professionals can play in the health of a community;
  • appreciation of the value of teachers and other community professionals in the development of healthy children and communities.

The Partners in Health Education Experience

The course consists of 11 commitments during the term, roughly one each week, though individual schedules vary greatly. Medical students meet cooperating teachers at an organizational session featuring a keynote presentation beneficial to both parties. Medical students arrange to observe the classes in which they will be teaching, and each medical student–teacher pair arranges a health education schedule for five teaching sessions over the course of the term. Eight to 16 medical students constitute the Partners seminar, which is led by a professor of pediatrics, a community health educator, and a teacher-trainer. The seminar meets three times during the term, with one session each toward its beginning, middle, and end. The exact schedule is a function of medical school exams, public school vacations, and other factors.

Each medical student is observed twice while teaching, ideally during the first and the third of the five lessons. A master teacher from the Upper Valley Teacher Training Program (UVTTP) works with the student on lesson preparation, videotapes the student teaching, and provides, together with the classroom teacher, feedback to the student immediately following these sessions. Written feedback from the teacher-trainer guides the student's home review of the videotape. At the end of the term, instructors, the program coordinator, student leaders, and medical student participants meet to generate written and oral feedback on the program. Teachers debrief the program with one or more of the instructors or teacher-trainers in person, on the phone, and through written evaluations.

Approximately 60 percent of the Partners graduates choose to continue teaching health in schools, most with their original cooperating teachers. Other students seek additional teaching experience with another Partners teacher in a different community or at a different grade level. Still other graduates participate in community-based activities of the medical school's Community Service Committee. All of these students have ongoing access to course faculty and resources.

Community Site Development

Schools within a 30-minute driving radius of the medical school were originally solicited for interest in the program through district and building administrators as well as individual teachers. Opinion leaders in each school have sustained participation and recruitment of cooperating teachers. Due to the elective nature of the course and the small class size at Dartmouth Medical School, much more demand for the program exists in the community than can be met by the program. Rural schools with fewer resources for health education are given preference in student placement, and students are clustered in schools with more than one cooperating teacher. Rarely is a medical student placed alone in a school. Teachers may request to participate in one or both terms of the program, matching their needs and schedules with those of the medical students.

The Partners faculty identify topical themes, such as "the human body," "nutrition and fitness," and "choices and health," in order to ensure coherence both in the medical student seminar and in lesson planning across all participants. However, within established themes, each medical student–teacher pair creates its own minicurriculum as defined by the interests of the medical student and the needs of the classroom. A cadre of veteran cooperating teachers now exists in core schools where medical students have taught for a number of years. A combination of new and experienced teachers is sought each year, and new schools have been added periodically, based on a school faculty's commitment, the availability of medical students, and coordination of schedules, topics, transportation, and other logistics. Partners graduates have responded to special requests of teachers or the Partners faculty in circumstances where a school's needs could not be met within the parameters of the Partners course.

Organization and Administration

The Partners in Health Education program was developed by the C. Everett Koop Institute at Dartmouth in close collaboration with the student-led Dartmouth Medical School Community Service Committee and local public schools. The Koop Institute sponsored and shepherded this innovation in the Dartmouth Medical School experience with support in part from the Helmut Schumann Foundation and a Learn and Serve America grant from the Corporation for National Service. Medical school faculty, a public school representative, a health education consultant, teacher-trainers, evaluators, and medical student representatives have shaped the program into its current form.

The half-time program coordinator serves as the principal contact for the program and course, functioning as one member of the course faculty and as leader of the resource development team. A teacher-trainer from the community-based Upper Valley Teacher Training Program serves as a second course instructor and coordinates the observation of student teaching, including the assimilation of feedback from master teachers and classroom teachers into the work of the seminar and the program. A professor of pediatrics completes the course faculty team, guiding the focus of the seminar for appropriate physician skill development. The three instructors structure the three 90-minute sessions for maximum benefit to the students in gaining mastery of developmentally appropriate teaching methods and messages, in planning lessons to effectively teach core messages, in problem solving around classroom issues, and in reflecting on the classroom experiences in light of clinical training, basic science course content, children's health issues, and other experiences.

One to four interested students have volunteered each year to serve as leaders for the following year's program. These second-year medical students participate in course planning, instruction, improvement efforts, student support, and evaluation efforts. They meet biweekly with the program coordinator and communicate regularly with student participants and course faculty in person and via electronic mail. All constituents participate in program improvement efforts through a variety of communication and feedback mechanisms. A comprehensive evaluation of the program and its effects provides summative assessment of program outcomes.

Resources and Support

Lesson development by students in Partners is guided by Teaching Frameworks — an approach that stratifies content in each topical theme into developmentally appropriate health messages. The Human Body, Nutrition and Fitness, and Choices and Health frameworks enable medical students to identify a core message, corresponding grade-specific messages, and useful teaching strategies for that grade. The frameworks have been developed by a team of health educators from the medical school and public school faculties, including the program coordinator. They are reviewed and updated annually.

Students also access lesson plans prepared by prior Partners students. The best of these are collected by the student leaders and circulated over electronic mail in a "tip of the week" series for students in the course. The program coordinator maintains a library of successful student lesson plans, comprehensive health education curricula, specialty resources, models, compact discs, and other teaching accessories.

Program Improvement and Feedback

Across its evolution, Partners in Health Education has existed in three distinctive formats, involving seven groups of medical students in more than 100 medical student–teacher pairs. Its evolution to the model elective course described here is largely due to participatory feedback and program responsiveness. Faculty, student leaders, and evaluators all constantly gather information and feedback on the program and apply them to the course in progress, the upcoming course, and longer-range planning for the program. The processes that are used to gather feedback include:

- two contacts per term between teacher-trainers and the program coordinator providing information on student performance in the schools;
- biweekly meetings of student leaders and the program coordinator on scheduling, seminar planning, teacher contacts, and medical student support;
- end-of-term oral and written feedback by medical students;
- an annual program evaluation by cooperating teachers;
- course faculty meetings before each term and before each seminar;
- ubiquitous access to and use of electronic mail by students and faculty;
- an annual program planning process that includes school representatives, student representatives, program faculty, and administrators;
- participation of program faculty in professional conferences and meetings on service-learning, participation of student leaders in local, regional, and national organizations on community service by medical students, participation of faculty in professional conferences and medical education improvement efforts, participation of evaluators in conferences and meetings.

Input from all of these external and internal sources is shared in regular team meetings and through program implementation contact.

The Partners in Health Education team is dedicated to the continuous improvement of the program so that it provides maximum benefit to the medical students, teachers, children, institutions, and communities participating in it.

Evaluation

The broad goals of the program and its potential importance to the participants, the community, and medical education demand an extensive evaluation of its many components.

Evaluation of Program Effects on Medical Students

The evaluation of the program's effects on participating medical students is guided by a model adapted from Bandura's theory of reciprocal determinism (1978). Utilization of this model describes the outcome of a service-learning situation as being the result of three features of the learning: the Person, the Environment, and the Behavior. The Person comprises what each participant brings with her or him into the service-learning experience, including attitudes, values, beliefs, previous experiences, skills, expectations, and other such characteristics. The Environment comprises the situation the participant encounters as he or she participates in the program, including any training curriculum, the characteristics of the location where the service is given, and other such features of the world in which the participant finds herself or himself during the time of service. The Behavior comprises the actual experiences the participant has and activities in which the participant engages during the program, including training, service activities, and other such behaviors.

The variety of evaluation instruments that have been used to assess the program's effects on participating medical students is based on earlier work by a project design team and on work published in the literature on medical education. We have administered an extensive core survey to the participants to gain an understanding of the personal histories and characteristics that play a role in the development of medical students during their education. We have administered a patient video interview both before and after the medical students have participated in the program. This interview is a video-based presentation of the cases of two patients that provides an opportunity for medical students to demonstrate their medical issue identification, goal-setting, and communication skills. Students at nine medical schools throughout the United States (including Dartmouth) have completed both the core survey and the patient video interview, which will enable us to compare students selecting the Partners program with classmates at Dartmouth and with students at the other comparison schools. Videotapes of Partners participants and other Dartmouth medical students in objective structured clinical exams — i.e., the interviewing of trained patient surrogates — will be reviewed to search for differences in communication skills that may result from the service-learning in the program.

In addition to using measures of student communication skills and program effects in medical settings, we have analyzed videotapes of students teaching their first and fourth lessons in the program in order to identify possible differences in the students' teaching behavior. Students have also completed pre- and postprogram surveys that assess expectations and perceptions of the program experience and learner characteristics. These surveys identify specific aspects of the program that are most salient and most responsible for the learning of the medical students.

Evaluation of Program Effects on Children

As a measure of both quality assurance and program effects, children in each participating class have been interviewed individually before and after the program to assess their perceptions of and attitudes toward health and health professionals. Comparison groups in the same school have been interviewed at the same time. The interviews were designed by examining the literature on how children develop attitudes and knowledge about health, by convening focus groups of teachers and health educators, and by discussing the program's impact on children with medical students who participated in Partners in previous years.

Analyses of Evaluation Findings

Some of the information we are collecting will not be available until the medical students are further along in their training. Other data are currently being analyzed. The analyses involve the collation of information from the varied sources into a relatively comprehensive view of the participants (the Person), the world in which they are learning (the Environment), and the activities that have resulted in some of the changes the medical students are experiencing (the Behavior). Our goal is to create a rich view of those medical students who choose to participate in service-learning, of the elements of the experience that contribute to its effects, and of the outcomes that result from such experiences. Early results indicate that medical students move from standing in front of the class and lecturing the students on health topics to sitting among the students and acting as a resource for the students to explore health topics as independent learners. We believe this change foreshadows similar important developments in the medical students' abilities to communicate with patients as clerks and in practice as physicians.

Lessons Learned

Service-learning program sustainability stems from providing students with an opportunity to develop skills that they find relevant and useful. This skill development must be matched with a need in the community and balanced with other academic demands placed on students. Sustainability through student, community, and faculty participation is a priority for service-learning programs in health professions schools. In our program, this has been accomplished through strong student leadership and meaningful collaboration. The Partners program utilizes existing community and health professions school resources in an efficient and effective manner. A program that does this, that is resource-effective and addresses the needs of all parties, instills in participants the motivation to sustain it. Some specific lessons learned include:

• The logistics of coordinating schedules, transportation, and resources is often not easy when programs as disparate as a medical school and an elementary school intersect; however, making the logistics simple for participants is critical to the success of the program.

• Student leadership is critical in any educational activity — especially in elective activities.

• Meaningful collaboration exists when all participants embrace the breadth of goals articulated by the team.

• Clear, regular, and frequent communication on all aspects of the program to all of its participants enhances collaboration and smooth implementation.

• The learning in service-learning occurs principally at the place of service. Providing support that gets students into that venue efficiently, such as model lesson plans and readily available teaching accessories, sustains their motivation and learning.

Partners in Health Education is a program that efficiently and effectively teaches relevant skills to first-year medical students in a community-based, nonclinical setting. Within weeks of beginning medical school, first-year students have skills that they recognize as being valuable to their learning experience in medical school and to their future careers as physicians. The Partners seminar prepares medical students to enter the classroom comfortably and with adequate skills so that their teaching experience is positive. In observing students develop through the program, however, and in listening to them reflect on their experience, we have been convinced that the children are the students' true teachers; we just help the students translate what they are being taught.

Reference

Bandura, A. (1978). "The Self System in Reciprocal Determinism." *American Psychologist* 33: 344-358.

Medical Students Go Back to Kindergarten:
Service-Learning and Medical Education in the Public Schools

by Kate Cauley, Elvira Jaballas, and Betty Holton

"A Healthy Child Is a Better Learner" is the name of the Learn and Serve America: Higher Education project launched in Dayton, Ohio. The project is administered through the Center for Healthy Communities (CHC), a community-academic partnership bringing together the Dayton Public Schools (DPS), public health and public housing, local hospitals, community health and mental health centers, health and human services organizations, Wright State University, and Sinclair Community College. Health professions students from the schools of Medicine and Professional Psychology, the College of Nursing and Health, and the Department of Social Work from Wright State and the departments of Dental Hygiene, Dietetic Technology, and Nursing from Sinclair are increasingly moving into community settings for their clinical training and education. Indeed, students are increasingly interested in opportunities to participate in a variety of community service activities, particularly when they can apply their developing knowledge and clinical skills. The project in Dayton matches the primary health-care needs of kindergarten children and their families with the health professions students' need for more community-based clinical training.

The medical school at Wright State University (WSU/SOM) has a long tradition of community-based clinical training and service. With no university hospital, its clinical training in tertiary-care institutions has from the beginning been sited at seven community-based hospitals. As a national leader in education of primary-care providers, WSU/SOM also has a history of clinical education and service in ambulatory care centers that are community-based. Several years ago, when looking to expand clinical training sites even further and to develop service-learning opportunities for medical students, WSU/SOM convened focus groups of community members — community leaders, providers, and consumers — to determine the best use of additional resources. In the Dayton Public Schools (DPS) system, a large number of children live at or below the poverty level, and approximately 73 percent of the student population is qualified for federal subsidies such as Aid to Dependent Children. Major sections of urban neighborhoods in Dayton, Ohio, are identified by the federal government as medically underserved. It was determined that one of the best places to send medical students would be into the public schools, where there was a captive and needy population of pediatric patients.

Medical school faculty and administrators began working with the DPS director of health services, 35 school nurses, and elementary school teachers. Six target schools were identified and plans begun to provide service for the children and clinical service-learning opportunities for undergraduate medical students. One of the primary concerns of DPS personnel was the number of children who did not have primary-care providers and consequently had not had a physical examination prior to enrolling in school as kindergartners. A system was developed that involved the school nurses' contacting parents of appropriate children and securing written permission for physical examinations. Parents were encouraged to be present for the examinations. Third-year ambulatory pediatric clerkship students were shifted from a community hospital site for one morning per week for periods of nine weeks in order to provide the examinations.

In order to increase the number of children being served, a second initiative was begun. For the Introduction to Clinical Medicine course for first-year students, a module was developed that focused on physical examinations of kindergarten-age children. Service teams consisting of four medical students, a physician, and the school nurse began providing physical examinations for kindergarten children for whom written parental permission had been obtained. Now, through these various efforts involving medical students, more than 100 medical students annually participate in these community-based clinical service-learning opportunities, and more than 100 kindergartners get their first physical examination.

In addition to the core curricular and clerkship service-learning opportunities described above, several elective courses have been developed involving medical students serving the community. In a summer course involving both medical and professional psychology students, students are trained to provide health and developmental screenings at kindergarten registration sites. During the school year, health professions students from all the disciplines provide health education to parent groups of DPS students, on topics from "How to Talk to Your Doctor/Psychologist" to stress management and healthy eating.

Prior to their public school service-learning experiences, medical students receive a full orientation to the Dayton Public Schools and its population of children, the urban community of Dayton, developmental issues of children of elementary school age, the Corporation for National Service, and issues related to cultural differences. Following the time of service and clinical training on-site in the public schools, medical students are given an opportunity to reflect on the experience both in terms of the technical learning experience and in terms of the experience of providing service to an underserved population. Students are also invited to reflect on ways to better serve the broader population of patients who are in the category of the urban poor. This initiative has proved quite successful. Indeed, the primary criticism has been that not enough health professions students are available to respond to the multiple requests for services.

Extensive evaluation of all student experiences has been completed. Overall, students evaluate the experiences quite favorably — 4.56 on a 5.0 scale. The most significant aspects of the experiences for the students included debunking stereotypical images of the urban poor, expanding their knowledge about health promotion and prevention services, increasing their knowledge of service-learning, and the hands-on nature of the learning experience. Evaluations have been completed by DPS personnel as well. Significantly, the service-learning program was invited back to the Dayton Public Schools for a third year.

The remainder of this article will review more extensively the development of service-learning in medical education at WSU/SOM. In addition, a review will also be provided of the development of the community-academic partnership that the Center for Healthy Communities represents. Finally, a reflective evaluation addressing lessons learned and ongoing challenges will be offered from the perspective of almost three years of experience with the program.

Community-Academic Partnerships

The Center for Healthy Communities (CHC) was initially supported by a grant from the Kellogg Foundation. Focused on improving primary health-care service delivery and health professions education in the Dayton community, one of the first tasks for the CHC was to establish the Community Advisory Board. Board membership included a wide range of community and academic leaders. Deans, associate deans, faculty, and students from the health professions schools, local government officials, public health officials, housing and school representatives, local hospital and community health center representatives, religious leaders, neighborhood leaders, and consumers of health-care services in the community were all enthusiastic participants. The Community Advisory Board sets overall policy and direction for the programs and activities of the CHC.

In addition to the Community Advisory Board, the governance structure of the center includes the Deans Advisory Committee and the Management Team. The Deans Advisory Committee, actually a subset of the Community Advisory Board, provides curricular and fiscal guidance for the CHC. The university serves as fiscal agent for the CHC, and the deans of the health professions schools ultimately determine the use of college, school, and department resources. The Management Team, which includes the center's director, all division directors, and the research associate, conducts the day-to-day business of the CHC. The five professional staff members and the seven community health advocates are aided by three administrative support staff. In addition, more than 50 health professions faculty members work directly with the CHC in developing and implementing multiprofessional and community-based health professions education and training curricula.

The work of the CHC is structured through four divisions — Community Health Advocacy, Community Health Development, Health Promotion, and Evaluation — and is guided by the following mission and goals:

Mission: *The Center for Healthy Communities is a community-academic partnership committed to improving the health and well-being of the community, educating its health-care professionals, and serving as a force for change.*

Goals:
1. *To develop strong partnerships and expand existing ones among community members, educators, and providers.*

2. *To educate students in the delivery of primary health care within our community.*

3. *To support and encourage community health advocacy and programs that empower community members to become active participants in their own health care and the health development of the community.*

4. *To develop new models of practice that incorporate a multidisciplinary team approach that is genuinely collaborative and cooperative.*

5. *To conduct and disseminate community-oriented health-care research designed to address specific health-care needs and problems.*

In order to improve primary health-care service delivery, the CHC began an extensive community assessment process. Through multiple focus groups and a review of earlier studies and reports, the CHC set about determining what barriers existed to full access and utilization of primary health-care services. Additionally, the strengths and needs of the community were assessed to determine where existing programs could best be supported and how, when gaps in services were found, the CHC could best respond.

One of the more important findings uncovered was the extent of the discomfort and distrust that existed in the community toward health-care delivery systems. Many of the urban poor in Dayton are African-American or Appalachian individuals who have had little to no experience with health-care services except through hospital emergency rooms. In large part, it is that inexperience that contributes to their feelings of discomfort. Breaking down natural barriers of unfamiliarity and inexperience seemed to be an important process to pursue. It became clear that one CHC initiative needed to be educating current and future providers about the wide diversity of patients in the community and educating consumers about services available to them. The Corporation for National Service initiative provided one opportunity to respond to these concerns.

Service-Learning in Medical Education

In order to improve the effectiveness of education in the health professions, a careful review of existing curricula was begun. Although each of the health professions schools participating in the CHC was already heavily involved in community-based clinical training and service, there was a demand for expanded sites with a stronger focus on learning to serve the poor. Providing more opportunities for planning, implementing, and evaluating primary health-care service delivery, increasing knowledge about community resources, and increasing cultural competence were all areas of emphasis for improved health professions student education and clinical training. Again, the Corporation for National Service initiative provided an important opportunity to respond to these concerns.

Corporation support through the CHC was primarily for faculty salary offsets and outreach workers in the community. Faculty from six different disciplines dedicated one day a week for a three-year period to the Corporation project. One of the primary goals of the project was to increase the number of health professions students at community-based sites utilized for clinical training and service. During the first year, the faculty team met weekly. In addition to faculty from the six health professions disciplines, team members included CHC staff responsible for community health advocacy and community health development, as well as the director of health services for the Dayton Public Schools. Simultaneously, faculty members began both an extensive faculty-development program and a curricular expansion effort.

The faculty-development component involved an initial reflection on all the various forms of service participants had experienced from the first time any of them was involved in community service to the present day. Among the group members were several former Girl and Boy Scouts who recalled early experiences in service to the community through scouting. Another participant had traveled across town to work as a candy striper at a local hospital and recalled the sense of independence she felt when working in this service capacity. Still others recalled experiences working in their neighborhoods through school or church. All had clear and vivid memories of these experiences and could easily articulate the personal relationship for them between early service experiences and professional vocation.

After some further study and reflections on community service opportunities in general and service-learning specifically, faculty team members developed broad service-learning objectives that would be applicable in any of the disciplines represented around the table. Next, discipline-specific and content-bound service-learning objectives were developed. The key was then to match the discipline-specific service-learning objectives with existing course offerings in each of the schools/departments, and begin planning opportunities for students to be in the community to complete their clinical training and provide service. The general service site had already been selected — the public school system. However, the kinds of services to be delivered and the training needs to be met had yet to be determined.

The Dayton Public Schools representative provided valuable information about the schools and the population of students served. Before pairs of service-learning faculty team members went out to meet with teachers, school nurses, and principals, they had developed some understanding of the social, economic, and cultural characteristics of the community and familiarity with the extensive health and human services already available to children in the public school system, and had learned about the challenges faced by the school system in areas such as immunization, timely school registration, completion of school physical examinations, and follow-ups to health and developmental screenings. Additionally, each health professions school established an agreement with the Dayton Public Schools — a contract articulating the nature of the relationship between the institutions, including standard liability clauses to protect health professions students and Dayton Public Schools children alike.

In Dayton, the public school system includes 35 elementary school buildings, six of which were targeted for participation in the Corporation initiative. Each elementary school had a school nurse and a large kindergarten population. At first, faculty team members tried meeting with large groups of teachers and nurses, briefing them about the initiative, and asking for suggestions about what health professions students could do. This generated a long list of concerns from teachers and nurses but seldom any clear ideas about what students could do to be of service.

The next step was for faculty team members to meet with individual teachers and school nurses at the target schools. These meetings were initially frustrating. School personnel saw this as one more thing to deal with. Project faculty were uncertain how best to use sites for service and training. However, as relationships were established and dialogue continued, ways to match the needs and interests of both the public schools and the health professions faculty and students began to emerge. For some faculty, the six target schools simply provided an expansion of existing community-based clinical sites. For others, the public schools were an entirely new venue for student service and training. For the WSU/SOM faculty and students, involvement with the public school system had been minimal prior to the Corporation initiative.

Fortunately, one of the faculty from the WSU/SOM, a pediatrician with a long history of service in the community, already had relationships established with several public school nurses. A way to involve students was quickly identified. The WSU/SOM faculty member regularly precepted third-year students in an ambulatory pediatric clerkship. One of the school nurses was system-wide coordinator of a state-wide initiative called Healthchek (more widely known nationally as Early Periodic Screening, Diagnostic, and Treatment). Medical students were released from their clerkship on Tuesday mornings to provide Healthchek physical examinations. The WSU/SOM faculty member, with the help of the Dayton Public Schools health services director and the school nurse, developed for the medical students an orientation to the community and the public schools. Parental permission and, when possible, participation in the Healthchek program were arranged through the school nurse. Follow-up to the physical examination was coordinated primarily through the school nurse, frequently with assistance from CHC outreach workers. Often the children had access to primary health care through one of several Medicaid managed-care groups in the community. However, sometimes parents were not aware they were eligible for the service, and at other times parents were actually enrolled in a plan but had not yet been to see their primary-care provider. A good deal of the follow-up work to ensure continuity of care was educational — helping people understand the services available to them and assisting them in making the link to those services.

The next service-learning opportunity was developed as a part of the first-year curriculum in the Introduction to Clinical Medicine course. Faculty had long been looking for a way to integrate direct service to children with the hands-on educational aspects of the course. Taking the medical students to the children in the public schools seemed the perfect solution. In groups of 45 to 50, medical students went to local elementary schools where school nurses and kindergarten teachers had obtained parental permission and established a system that facilitated physical examinations for children who did not have primary-care providers. Teams of four students and one faculty member worked with groups of four kindergarten children. The hands-on experience was fun and beneficial for all. Children received a physical examination, learned how to use a stethoscope, and interacted with each other, the physician, and the medical students. Medical students received an excellent hands-on opportunity to learn about the pediatric physical examination, interacting with the children and gaining important experience. Follow-up services were coordinated through both the school nurses and local providers. Initially, follow-up services had not been specifically included. However, on the first day of the first class, one of the CHC community health advocates (outreach workers) confronted the chair of the Department of Family Medicine with this question: "What are you going to do for these children when you find something wrong?" Now procedures are in place to link families with available resources in the community and in some cases to refer them to clinics staffed by WSU/SOM faculty and students.

About six months into the program, enough of a preliminary relationship had been established between the health professions schools and the public school system to facilitate specific requests from school personnel for service. One of the first of these was a request for health professions students to provide health education workshops and seminars for Dayton Public Schools parents through the Title I parent education program. More than 20 health professions students participated that first year. Three years later, there are routinely close to 40 health professions students involved annually, staffing an entire day of health education offerings for community members. Medical students have provided a variety of programs, from "What's Up Doc?" — a workshop for parents on the kinds of things for which one should seek a physician's care — to the "Teddy Bear Clinic" — a workshop for children about personal hygiene and infection control. Other requests have come for assistance with kindergarten registration and health screenings, follow-up referrals and services for deficiencies identified through hearing, vision, and developmental screenings, and assistance with school immunizations. In response to these latter requests, selective courses for medical students have been developed that include an orientation component, field-based service-learning, and a reflective component.

Reflective Evaluation

Each year the opportunities for health professions students in the public schools have expanded. All three service-learning opportunities in medical education — the third-year ambulatory pediatric clerkship, the first-year Introduction to Clinical Medicine course, and the elective courses — are now a routine part of the curriculum. More than 20 WSU/SOM faculty and 150 students participate in service-learning opportunities annually. The challenges that remain have been with the program from the beginning, and have diminished slightly each year, but in many ways are timeless and will continue to demand attention in the future. For example, traditional town-gown conflicts are always in the background, regardless of strong individual relationships between medical school faculty and public school personnel.

Indeed, whenever a nurse is moved to another school or a new teacher comes on board or a new faculty member joins the service-learning team, whenever a new class of students enters, there are opportunities for growth as well as challenges to the established order.

For health professions schools with a tradition of community-based clinical training, the most significant challenge has been distinguishing regular clinical training opportunities from service-learning experiences. This has not been entirely resolved at the CHC. To date, however, several conclusions have been reached. First, the Corporation initiative has clearly expanded the clinical training and service sites in use. Students have moved into nontraditional arenas and are finding excellent opportunities at sites that have not traditionally provided health-care or health education services. Second, service-learning community-based clinical training opportunities are distinguished by a structured orientation to the patient population and community site prior to site-based work. Third, service-learning experiences are distinguished by a structured reflective component providing students with an opportunity to integrate the concepts of training and service. Finally, service-learning experiences assume an effort on the part of the health professions faculty to intentionally shift the focus of the training experience toward service.

Expanding somewhat on the work of Andrew Furco, specifically his article in *Expanding Boundaries* (1996), the CHC has developed a graphical representation of the emphasis on service and learning for various kinds of applied educational experiences. This tool is useful for both academic and community partners in the service-learning program. For health professions faculty, such an experiential education graph is part of a larger faculty-development presentation called "Enhancing the Learning Environment: Learning the Language of Experiential Education." Faculty who are interested in developing a service-learning component for their courses or clinical training programs can use the graph as a standard by which to gauge their success. For community members and agency staff, the graph is part of a larger presentation called "Accessing the Resources of Higher Education." Community agency staff who are likely to use students are given an opportunity to review the focus, type of experience, faculty role, and agency role for various kinds of experiential learning.

The increased numbers of students in the community and in particular in the public schools have posed challenges for the community as well. There are two universities and one community college in Dayton and several other institutions within 50 miles of the city. As cooperative education, experiential learning, applied education, field experiences, community service, servant leadership, and service-learning enjoy a renewed life in higher education, the community in which services are provided is saying it is confused, overwhelmed, and sometimes frustrated. Hence, it is asking for several things. First, a single point of entry into each educational institution would be helpful. There needs to be one telephone number for each institution that anyone in the community can call to get information about where students are placed or would like to be placed. Second, community organizations want to better understand the various levels of student involvement/availability. Are students available for the entire semester, just one day, or multiple times during the quarter? What are the expectations of universities/colleges with regard to supervision of students' work? Third, community organizations are asking how they can better communicate the nature of the work they want done so that faculty members will be interested in their organization and direct the appropriate-level student to assist.

In response, the CHC has established the Service-Learning Advisory Committee (SLAC). SLAC meets quarterly and brings together representatives from all three Dayton institutions of higher education, the Miami Valley Association of Volunteer Administrations, staff from multiple health and human services agencies, and faculty and students to better coordinate the work of matching student interests and talents with community needs. CHC also has developed and regularly provides to community agency staff seminars on how to write job descriptions and how to write learning objectives to accompany those job descriptions. Furthermore, it has developed workshops to assist faculty in writing service-learning objectives and in learning how to better integrate service-learning into their curriculum. Twice annually, a survey is sent to community organizations requesting information about opportunities for students in the coming months. Once a year, faculty are surveyed to gather information about their curricular service-learning interests. Finally, SLAC is working to better coordinate and monitor service-learning activities for health professions students throughout the entire region.

Yet despite all these efforts, the multiprofessional component of the Corporation initiative has been only moderately successful. To some extent, this is due to the fact that the program is new and each discipline has had to focus internally before it could focus on integrated experiences for multiple disciplines. However, to some extent, coordinating levels of student training and expertise, schedules, and faculty available for precepting students across multiple disciplines will continue to be a major challenge for the foreseeable future. To be sure, there have been some notably successful multiprofessional experiences. Medical and professional psychology students teamed up to help with physical and developmental screenings for kindergarten children. Nursing and dietetic technology students have worked together on health-risk appraisals. Dietetic technology students have worked with medical students and school nurses to provide education and

Healthcheks in the elementary schools. All of the professions have planned and worked together for the Title I parent education classes. But even more important to the overall success of the program has been the multiprofessional faculty involvement facilitated through the Learn and Serve faculty team. Opportunities for exchanges with health professions colleagues and for developing, with assistance from colleagues in multiple disciplines, new clinical training and service sites have been useful and rewarding experiences for all the faculty involved in the program.

Conclusion

Having laid the foundation for community-academic partnerships through the Center for Healthy Communities, and with initial fiscal support from the Corporation for National Service, service-learning in medical education at Wright State University has caught on in a big way. Though there are always new lessons to be learned, with every new challenge the program improves. Service-learning in medical education — as a regular part of the core curriculum through the Introduction to Clinical Medicine course for the first-year undergraduates, a regular component of the ambulatory pediatric clerkship rotation for third-year students, and the basis for a number of elective courses each year — is now a significant part of the medical student experience at Wright State University. Each year, students and faculty in consultation with the community develop innovative ways to combine — through service-learning — the needs of the community with the education and training needs of health professions students.

Reference

Furco, A. (1996). "Service-Learning: A Balanced Approach to Experiential Education." In *Expanding Boundaries: Service and Learning,* edited by J. Raybuck, pp. 2-6. Washington, DC: Corporation for National Service.

Service-Learning in Medical Education:
Teaching Psychiatry Residents How to Work With the Homeless Mentally Ill

by Richard C. Christensen

In 1989, a free primary-care clinic for the homeless in Gainesville, Florida, was established through the voluntary efforts of a nurse practitioner and a hospital social worker. It was based at a local shelter for the homeless located in the downtown area. Established to meet the primary-care needs of the homeless and poor in the community, the Helping Hands Clinic for the Homeless continues to operate one night per week and is staffed by health-care providers consisting of nurses, physician assistants, and primary-care physicians.

A community service model based at this clinic was initiated in 1991 by two residents (one of whom is the author) and a faculty member affiliated with the Department of Psychiatry at the University of Florida. Responding to the expressed need of the clinic supervisors, who identified a significant number of homeless individuals whose psychiatric disorders were not being adequately treated, these three offered to provide service to homeless individuals who frequented the Helping Hands Clinic. As a consequence, the two trainees and one faculty member agreed to make available their services, on a rotating basis, in order to evaluate and treat patients at the clinic. At that time, the clinical work was strictly service-oriented. No one had any intention of incorporating it into the residency training curriculum.

Over the course of the following two years, only I continued to provide weekly care at the clinic. However, the number of individuals seeking evaluation and treatment grew as word spread that free psychiatric care was being offered at the site. In 1993, after recognizing that the community's need was greater than a single psychiatrist could meet, I made an active attempt to recruit fellow psychiatry residents to serve one night a month at the clinic. Two residents responded, but over the course of several months, their participation waned and finally ceased altogether. In truth, resident participation in this model of community service did not increase until the activity was formally recognized by the department as an educationally based component of the residency training program.

Today at the University of Florida, psychiatry residents have a unique opportunity to learn how to care for the homeless mentally ill. Residents who participate in this voluntary educational activity not only provide direct community service to a significantly underserved population but also learn about the context in which the service is provided through a series of seminars supplemented by appropriate readings. This paper will describe how this experience in community service has evolved into a core educational component of the department's Community Mental Health Program. My intention is to illustrate the potentially valuable role community service experiences can play in meeting both the educational needs of the resident and the health-care needs of a community. Although this particular model of community service is specific to a psychiatry residency program, the lessons learned from its design and implementation are no doubt applicable to training programs within other medical specialties.

Service as a Response to Community Need

Over the course of the past decade, the estimated number of homeless persons in this country has ranged from 500,000 to 1.9 million (Brickner et al. 1993). The most recent studies, however, place the figure at nearly 600,000, with approximately one-third of this number manifesting signs of severe mental illness (e.g., schizophrenia, bipolar affective disorder, and major depression) (Bachrach 1992). Access to mental health care for members of this population is fraught with obstacles. Lack of income and health-care insurance, inability to negotiate complex community mental health systems, and mistrust of mental health care providers are just a few of the more obvious impediments the homeless confront in obtaining psychiatric care (Interagency Council 1992). Those who provide care to this population usually do so in nontraditional clinical settings: shelters, streets, bus stations, city parks, and even public restrooms. Clinicians who engage and assess the homeless mentally ill must be prepared to modify many of the traditional expectations surrounding the doctor-patient relationship. As a consequence, psychiatrists who serve this special population require a body of knowledge, a set of attitudes, and an armamentarium of clinical skills that are not easily acquired in the conventional clinical setting (Susser, Valencia, and Goldfinger 1992).

The city of Gainesville has a population of approximately 96,000. Although there are no exact figures, an unpublished study conducted by the Gainesville Comprehensive Housing Affordability Strategy (CHAS) in 1992 placed the number of homeless in the community at between 600 and 700 on any given night. The routes to homelessness are many, but the most widely accepted paths for the mentally ill are deinstitutionalization, lack of affordable housing, lack of linkages among service-delivery systems, inadequate discharge planning from mental health facilities, and disaffiliation from familial support systems (Bachrach 1992; Interagency Council 1992). All of these factors to one degree or another play a role in contributing to the number of mentally ill living on the streets of Gainesville. Although the precise number of homeless mentally ill in the community is unknown, one can offer an educated guess, based on the national research finding that approximately one-third of all homeless individuals suffer from a serious mental illness. Hence, the number of mentally ill persons who are living on the streets in Gainesville can be estimated to be between 200 and 250.

The Evolution of Service Into a Residency Training Activity

This particular educational model of service to the homeless gradually became a part of the residency training curriculum in 1994 when I became a faculty member and director of the department's newly established Community Mental Health Program. The model assumed a recognizable position in the residency training curriculum when it was officially placed under the auspices of the Community Mental Health Program. As part of that program's educational agenda, a number of presentations were made to the residents that focused on both the local and the national issues of homelessness. One lecture in particular was a Grand Rounds presentation to the entire department that specifically identified the need for mental health care among the local homeless population. As a result of this underscoring of the local community need in a formal way, together with the availability of an identifiable faculty member and a departmental program that had the potential to impact immediately an underserved population, eight residents stepped forward to offer their services.

Departmental recognition by the Department of Community Service as an accepted educational activity was also solidified in other ways. An agreement was reached with the residency training director and the faculty supervisor of the Adult Outpatient Psychiatry Clinic that allowed the residents who treated patients at the shelter-based clinic to formally count these individuals as part of their outpatient caseload. Residents were permitted to record the patients they treated at the clinic in their monthly patient logs, and I assumed a clinical supervisory role for these residents in their service to homeless outpatients.

It is noteworthy that members of the department other than residents also began participating in this particular community service experience. Over the course of the past few years, several faculty members have offered their time to provide direct supervision at the clinic. In addition, a number of nurse practitioners and physician assistants affiliated with the department have offered their services on an intermittent basis.

At the present time, residents serve one night per month at the clinic. On average, they will see approximately two to three patients for initial evaluations, medication management, and/or brief supportive therapy. After seeing a particular patient, they will discuss their assessment with the faculty member who is supervising the clinic on that particular night. The faculty member and resident will then meet with the patient to discuss treatment options and appropriate follow-up measures. The types of patients seen span the spectrum of psychiatric diagnoses. In general, however, the three most common diagnostic entities are adjustment disorders, major depression, and schizophrenia. The vast majority of these individuals also exhibit signs of comorbid substance use disorders.

Close interaction between residents and faculty members not only ensures a high quality of care for the individuals being treated but also creates an exceptional educational opportunity to teach clinical skills that are especially relevant to working effectively with the homeless mentally ill. Uniting attending faculty member and resident in this collegial educational relationship is the unspoken awareness that they are providing care to those who would otherwise go untreated. It can reasonably be argued that it is this component of the experience that has the potential to influence profoundly a resident's attitudes toward the value and purposefulness of community service.

Integration of Service With Reflection: Establishing a Seminar Series

During 1995, I met bimonthly in a group with the residents who were involved in the community service program. Although faculty provided a direct supervisory component in the clinical setting, there was little time during those clinical hours to discuss the more theoretical causes and effects of homelessness. Moreover, the pace of the clinical setting prevented a more reflective assessment of the value of the clinical work or the purpose of community service in graduate medical education. Hence, the primary objective of these initial meetings was to add a formal reflection component to the actual clinical service.

The initial meetings were relatively unstructured in format. However, a paper dealing with an issue related to health care for the homeless was usually discussed. These bimonthly meetings served two purposes. First, they allowed residents the opportunity to identify and articulate the concrete issues they were confronting in their community service experience at the clinic. Second, they helped add to the experience a formal academic component that could underscore the more fundamental and theoretical issues behind provision of psychiatric care to the homeless mentally ill. In other words, this component was designed to provide a context within which residents could achieve a broader understanding of the core issues related to their work with a profoundly underserved population.

Since then, the model of action-reflection just described has been developed into a monthly seminar series entitled Topics in Community Psychiatry and offered to all residents. The series includes such topics as psychiatry and the homeless mentally ill (Morse et al. 1996), mental illness among homeless women (Smith and North 1993), dual diagnosis within the homeless population (Levine and Huebner 1991), HIV and the homeless mentally ill (Susser, Valencia, and Goldfinger 1992), and ethical issues in the clinical care of the homeless (Christiansen n.d.). Over the years, it became apparent that a number of residents who were unable to provide direct service to the homeless were nonetheless interested in learning more about providing health care to this vulnerable population. To establish a formal seminar series has been driven, therefore, by several different kinds of resident interest. Almost alone among curriculum initiatives — typically limited to a specific postgraduate year — the community service program (i.e., both its clinical and academic components) remains available to all residents, regardless of their year of residency.

Evaluation

Evaluation consists of an assessment by each participating resident of the overall quality of the service experience as well as the efficacy of faculty supervision. An assessment of each resident's performance by the director of the Community Mental Health Program has, of course, also been instituted.

Informal feedback from the residents is elicited at the monthly seminar series to identify elements of the service experience (e.g., on-site clinical work, clinical supervision by faculty, extent of patient care responsibilities, didactics, etc.) that need to be modified or strengthened. Residents provide written evaluations of the quality of the educational experience, including the quality and quantity of faculty supervision, at the end of the academic year. A formal evaluation of each resident's performance is completed at the same time and is placed in the individual's academic file.

. In general, evaluation of the service experience by the residents has been highly favorable, and this response is reflected in the increasing number both of trainees and of faculty who have asked to participate. Although residents undertake their service on an elective basis, more than one-third of the residents in the Department of Psychiatry (13 of 36) participate in the program. Also of note is the fact that at least one resident from each year of training (e.g., PGY-1 through PGY-4) is currently involved.

Community Service: Achieving Mutual Educational and Community Goals

This particular model of community service at the residency training level aims to achieve a number of educational goals that are simultaneously beneficial to the community. First, community service experiences in residency training provide physicians with an opportunity to learn, firsthand, the depth and the extent of the health-care needs of underserved communities. Residents are given an opportunity to practice in a clinical environment (e.g., a shelter-based clinic) and to treat a population of patients (e.g., the homeless mentally ill) they might otherwise not encounter in an academic medical setting. Second, having physicians engage in community service (as distinct from opportunities involving medical students) usually translates into improved access to mental health care resources for underserved populations. Due to their level of training in postgraduate medical education, residents have the capacity to assess, diagnose, and actually treat a number of patients under the supervision of a faculty member. In general, this creates a variety of accessible pathways for individuals to be seen by a physician who can assume primary responsibility for their care. Third, it has been noted that one responsibility of medical schools and their training programs is to incorporate a sense of the social contract into the medical education of physicians (Fisher 1995; Poulsen 1995). This particular model of community service at the residency training level has the capacity to cultivate within the training physician a deepened sense of social responsibility and activism, particularly with regard to those who are least well off. Finally, elective community service opportunities in residency have the potential to enliven and enhance the altruistic attitudes and inclinations with which residents first entered the medical educational system.

Recommendations for Implementing Community Service Opportunities

The Department of Psychiatry at the University of Florida College of Medicine has successfully integrated a model of service-learning education into its residency training program. Several factors, however, were critical to the design and implementation of this unique educational opportunity. Other graduate medical education programs, regardless of their particular specialty (e.g., family medicine, pediatrics, obstetrics-gynecology, etc.), that are thinking of including a community service experience as part of their residency training should consider the following recommendations:

1. *Select a training site (e.g., a shelter-based clinic for the homeless) that meets*

both the needs of the community and the educational goals of the residency training program. Identifying community need is the first and perhaps most important step in developing a community-based service opportunity for resident physicians. Contacting local social service agencies, nonprofit organizations, free clinics, shelters, and other service providers in the community is an excellent way of assessing community health needs. Of equal importance, however, is identifying the educational gaps that currently exist in the residency program (e.g., lack of familiarity with community-based sites, ambulatory care settings, rural environments, etc.) and developing an initiative that seeks to meet these resident training needs.

2. "Institutionalize" the community service as an educational activity by establishing a formal relationship with the department's residency training program. Not all community service opportunities are perceived by residents and faculty as being of equal educational value. For example, at the University of Florida, it was not until community service was officially recognized as a legitimate educational activity by the residency training office, even though involvement remained voluntary, that residents began to participate on a regular basis.

3. Recruit supervising faculty members with a demonstrated commitment to teaching and an appreciation of the value of community service. Central to the successful implementation of service experiences in residency training is the involvement of faculty who are both excellent teachers and committed to the ideals of community service in medical education. A capacity to teach in clinical settings outside the traditional boundaries of an academic medical center, as well as an ability to cultivate a heightened awareness of a particular community's health-care needs, is essential for the faculty member who participates as a resident supervisor.

4. Provide trainees with a well-supervised learning environment and a formal component of reflection.

5. Establish an evaluation system that is specific and timely, and assesses all components of the community service experience.

Conclusion

Medical schools and residency training programs are being urged to modify their educational practices and agendas in order to produce physicians who are more responsive to the health-care needs of the society in which they practice (Eckhert 1995; Welch and Fisher 1992). Training residents to be more knowledgeable about, and responsive to, the health-care needs of their communities ought to be an educational goal of all training programs. Service opportunities in residency training programs can play a critical role in meeting this challenging educational and social need.

References

Bachrach, L.L. (1992). "What We Know About Homelessness Among Mentally Ill Persons: An Analytical Review and Commentary." *Hospital and Community Psychiatry* 43(5): 453-464.

Brickner, P.W., J.M. McAdam, R.A. Torres et al. (1993). "Providing Health Services for the Homeless: A Stitch in Time." *Bulletin of the New York Academy of Medicine* 70(3): 146-167.

Christensen, R.C. (n.d.). "Ethical Issues in the Clinical Care of the Homeless Mentally Ill." Unpublished manuscript.

Eckhert, N.L. (1995). "Training Caregivers to Be More Responsive to Their Communities." *Academic Medicine* 70(7): 564.

Fisher, H.M. (1995). "Community Service as an Integral Component of Undergraduate Medical Education: Facilitating Student Involvement." *Bulletin of the New York Academy of Medicine* 72(1): 76-86.

Interagency Council on the Homeless. (1992). *Outcasts on Main Street: Report of the Federal Task Force on Homelessness and Severe Mental Illness.* Washington, DC: Interagency Council on the Homeless.

Levine, I.S., and R.B. Huebner. (1991). "Homeless Persons With Alcohol, Drug, and Mental Disorders." *American Psychologist* 46: 1113-1114.

Morse, G.A., R.J. Calsyn, J. Miller et al. (1996). "Outreach to Homeless Mentally Ill People: Conceptual and Clinical Considerations." *Community Mental Health Journal* 32: 261-274.

Poulsen, E.J. (1995). "Student-Run Clinics: A Double Opportunity." *Journal of the American Medical Association* 273: 430.

Smith, E.M., and C.S. North. (1993). "Not All Homeless Women Are Alike: Effects of Motherhood and the Presence of Children." *Community Mental Health Journal* 30: 601-610.

Susser, E. (1996). "Injection Drug Use and Risk of HIV Transmission Among Homeless Men With Mental Illness." *American Journal of Psychiatry* 153: 794-798.

——— , E. Valencia, and S.M. Goldfinger. (1992). "Clinical Care of Homeless Mentally Ill Individuals: Strategies and Adaptations." In *Treating the Homeless Mentally Ill: A Task Force Report of the American Psychiatric Association,* edited by H.R. Lamb, L.L. Bachrach, and F.L. Kass, pp. 127-140. Washington, DC: APA Press.

Welch, H.G., and E.S. Fisher. (1992). "Let's Make a Deal: Negotiating a Settlement Between Physicians and Society." *New England Journal of Medicine* 327: 1312-1315.

An Interdisciplinary Service-Learning Community Health Course for Preclinical Health Sciences Students

by Daniel Blumenthal, Meryl S. McNeal, Lorine Spencer, JoAnne Rhone, and Fred Murphy

This paper describes the philosophy, development, implementation, and evaluation of an interdisciplinary, community-based service-learning course in community health. The course was developed as one component of the Community Partnerships for Health Professions Education project funded by the W.K. Kellogg Foundation through a grant to Morehouse School of Medicine (MSM). The other health sciences schools that have participated in the course are the Georgia State University School of Nursing and both the School of Social Work and the Allied Health Department at Clark-Atlanta University.

Morehouse School of Medicine is a private, predominantly black school whose mission is to produce primary-care physicians for careers in medically underserved communities. Clark-Atlanta University is also a private, predominantly black institution. Georgia State University is a public institution that trains nurses for service to the needy.

Course Elements

The goal of the course described here is to enable students to analyze the health problems of a defined community, and design and implement interventions to address those problems. The course was developed according to the following principles:

1. The special health problems of minorities, the poor, and residents of underserved communities are more likely to respond to a community-based or population-based approach that emphasizes prevention than to an approach based on the treatment of individual patients or clients.

2. Health professionals working in underserved areas must have the knowledge, skills, and attitudes to work in and with communities, particularly since there may be few other health workers with whom to share responsibility for the health of the community.

3. The community cannot be used as a "learning laboratory"; rather, it must be engaged in a partnership that enables student learning at the same time that service is rendered to the community.

The course meets one half-day per week throughout the academic year. It is required of all first-year medical students at Morehouse and all community health nursing majors at Georgia State, and replaces required didactic classes. It is an elective for Clark-AU social work and allied health students. The course coordinator is a member of the MSM faculty.

The course calls for dividing the class into small groups, each consisting of about 10 students (typically four medical students, four nursing students, one social work student, and one allied health student). Each group is assigned to a community, usually working under the auspices of a local community organization. Two faculty members (to allow for circumstances in which one must be absent) are assigned to lead the group, the community organization assigns a liaison, and a biostatistician or epidemiologist is available as necessary for assistance with data analysis. Each group meets in a community center, a community clinic, or other local facility. When the entire class must meet together (for instance, for the introductory session), the large meeting room of a community health center is used.

Thus, the course is more resource-intensive in terms of both faculty time and community facilities than is a traditional lecture-based course. Moreover, it requires considerable faculty development, since the ability to effectively direct small groups of students in community activities is not a skill most faculty possess. Faculty-development sessions have been conducted by experienced faculty with assistance from the Southeastern Primary Care Consortium (SPCC), a community corporation that serves as a link between the community and academic institutions (see discussion below). Community partners, in turn, are all expected to assign liaison representatives to work closely with the faculty to ensure that students achieve the course objectives.

The first semester is devoted to conducting a community health needs assessment, which may include door-to-door surveys, meetings with community leaders, visits to local health-care facilities, focus groups, and analysis of secondary data from the health department or other sources. At the end of the semester, the students present their findings in a public hearing format to a panel of state legislators and other policymakers in a hearing room at the state capital. During the second semester, each group of students designs and implements one or more health promotion interventions that address community needs identified during the first semester. Each semester's work is summarized in a group paper.

Interactions Among Students of Different Disciplines

The course format requires students to work together in interdisciplinary teams. Seventy-five percent of the grade is based on the quality of projects and papers developed by the students as a group. In order to complete these activities, students must work together outside class as well as during class hours. They must learn to compromise, support one another, and rely on their teammates.

Some authors suggest that students should be introduced to other members of the health-care team early in their development (Headrick et al. 1996; World Health Organization 1988), whereas others recommend that this should take place after the students have developed their professional skills (Kindig 1975). We have, in fact, found that the point in a student's educational program at which he or she takes our course does affect his or her relationship with other health professions students. Medical students enroll in the course as freshmen and take it concurrently with biochemistry, physiology, and gross anatomy. These students have often remarked that the course should be less demanding than their basic science courses and have resisted spending a great deal of time on it. The nursing students, by contrast, are usually seniors in a BSN program and regard the course as a capstone experience. They have often resented the reluctance of some of the medical students to perform their share of the teamwork. Most often, however, they have been successful in persuading the medical students to participate more fully.

The master's-level social work students have been well schooled in the teamwork tradition of their profession; they generally enjoy the opportunity to function as a member of a student team. Like the social work students, the allied health students are enrolled in the course on an elective basis, and also generally enjoy the opportunity to interact with students of other health professions.

Communities and the Community Partnership

The course has been developed in collaboration with several Atlanta communities with which the schools had established partnerships over the preceding two to four years. An important link between the academic institutions and many of these communities was the Southeastern Primary Care Consortium, a new 501(c)(3) corporation that was established for this purpose. The board of directors of the SPCC comprises both academy and community representatives, with the latter in the majority. The SPCC employs a small staff, which is responsible for organizing communities around health-related issues and helping to establish community coalitions that can undertake health promotion activities (Braithwaite et al. 1989). These coalitions may themselves become incorporated in order to pursue independent funding, with the assistance of the SPCC and/or the academic partners.

The coalitions typically represent communities of 3,000 to 5,000 low-income inner-city African Americans. The communities have high rates of morbidity and social problems, but they also have important assets, including clinics, senior citizen centers, community centers, schools, and churches. Taking inventory of these assets is often part of the students' needs-assessment process, and publicizing them may be part of an intervention.

Community Health Needs Assessment

Our approach to conducting a community health needs assessment and developing health promotion interventions is based on the PRECEDE/ PROCEED model developed by Greene and Kreuter (1991). The assessment usually begins with a "windshield survey" (walk-through or drive-through of the community) (Anderson and McFarland 1988; Clark 1992). This is followed by a review of census data, health statistics from the county health department, data from the housing authority (if the community is a public housing project), and other sources of statistical information. Students also interview community leaders regarding local issues of importance. Examples of community leaders include the president of the local neighborhood planning unit (part of the city zoning apparatus), the principal of the neighborhood school, the director of a day-care center, ministers, public health nurses, and businessmen.

Using these sources of information, the students may decide to develop a questionnaire and conduct a house-to-house survey for more detailed quantitative information, and/or they may decide to conduct focus groups to gather more extensive qualitative information. They may follow these activities by conducting a SWOT (strengths, weaknesses, opportunities, threats) analysis.

Survey data are analyzed using EPI-INFO software. The information accumulated is developed into a paper that offers suggestions for local action, as well as policy or legislative recommendations. This paper is presented to a panel of legislators and other policymakers in a mock public hearing at the state capital. Legislators who have participated in this exercise have acknowledged that it was a policy-relevant learning experience for them.

Interventions

The students' health promotion interventions have necessarily been limited in scope, as the time that the students are able to devote to these projects is generally limited. The most common activities have been health fairs and educational presentations, often involving children or youth.

Perhaps one of the most important questions, from a service-learning perspective, is the extent to which students' activities have resulted in a lasting impact on the community. This has been highly variable. An example of an activity with such an impact is a Narcotics Anonymous chapter that was established by students in response to the identification of drug abuse as an important community problem. By contrast, another group of students responded to community environmental concerns by cleaning up the trash and broken glass in a neighborhood vacant lot. Within a few weeks, the lot was again full of trash. Even in the latter case, however, the students had established their eagerness to contribute to the community rather than just to learn from it. The next year, another group of students was welcomed back by the community coalition.

Evaluation and Lessons Learned

Student evaluation of the course has been obtained through anonymous questionnaires at the end of each semester. During the two years that the course has been offered in the current format, about 65 percent of the students have rated the small-group experiential service-learning approach "good" to "excellent." About a third of the medical students indicated that they preferred the lecture approach.

Evaluation by our community partners was more informal. Conversations with community leaders elicited great enthusiasm for the student projects and requests that these projects continue. Of 11 communities participating in the course during a two-year period, only one expressed dissatisfaction such that we did not return the next year.

Analysis of our experiences suggests the following lessons:

• There is no "best" time to introduce students to other members of the interdisciplinary team. Students will learn from and about one another regardless of their level of training.

• Students nearly all "buy into" the course ethic and strive to contribute something lasting to the community rather than merely working for a grade. Some students have suggested that their projects be taken up by future classes, others have elected to continue working in the communities, and others have prepared grant proposals.

• Interdisciplinary faculty must provide students with an exemplary model of teamwork. If students perceive conflict among the faculty, they are likely to emulate this behavior in their own interdisciplinary groups.

• An interdisciplinary service-learning course requires a reliable time commitment from faculty, substantial faculty development for those who have little or no community or small-group experience, and continual marketing to noninvolved faculty (and curriculum committees) who may have confidence only in traditional teaching methods.

• In view of the greater faculty commitment of time and effort this mode of teaching requires, adequate institutional recognition and rewards must be assured. Such recognition is usually not granted under traditional methods of faculty evaluation; a more qualitative approach must be used that takes the faculty's additional time commitment into account.

References

Anderson, E.T., and J. McFarland. (1988). *Community as Client: Application of the Nursing Process.* Philadelphia, PA: Lippincott.

Braithwaite, R.L., F. Murphy, N. Lythcott, and D.S. Blumenthal. (1989). "Community Organization and Development for Health Promotion Within an Urban Black Community: A Conceptual Model." *Health Education* 20(5): 56-60.

Clark, M.J. (1992). *Nursing in the Community.* Hartford, CT: Appleton and Lange.

Greene, L., and M. Kreuter. (1991). *Health Promotion Planning: An Educational and Environmental Approach.* Mountain View, CA: Mayfield.

Headrick, L.A., L. Norman, S. Gelmon, and M. Knapp. (1996). *Interdisciplinary Professional Education in the Continuous Improvement of Health Care: The State of the Art.* Final Report. Order No. 103HR940534P000-000. Rockville, MD: Health Resources and Services Administration, Bureau of Health Professions.

Kindig, D. (1975). "Interdisciplinary Education for Primary Health Care Team Delivery." *Journal of Medical Education* 50: 97-110.

World Health Organization. (1988). *Learning to Work Together for Health.* Technical Report Series No. 769. Geneva, Switzerland: WHO.

Service-Learning Opportunities at the Ohio State University: The Community Medicine Rotation and the Community Project

by Franklin R. Banks and Catherine A. Heaney

This article provides a description of two programs at the Ohio State University that offer service-learning opportunities for medical students. The Community Medicine Rotation is an elective program for third- and fourth-year medical students. The Community Project is a required program for all first-year medical students. This article presents information regarding the goals, structure, and service components of these two programs.

The Community Medicine Rotation

Since 1971, the Community Medicine Rotation at the Ohio State University has offered opportunities for third- and fourth-year medical students to participate in varied field assignments. To date, medical students have participated in some 2,500 field assignments. These assignments have been located in Ohio (69.1%), in 43 other states in the United States (25.2%), and in 48 other countries (5.7%). Assignments, which are full-time and for a minimum of four weeks, provide students with opportunities to study the nature and magnitude of human health problems and the means by which societies cope with them. They also provide opportunities for students to explore varied career options. Many of these assignments have given students opportunities to work with medically underserved populations in a variety of field settings in both rural and urban areas. Students have engaged in service projects of value to their host agencies and the communities that those agencies serve.

Students have participated in assignments in a wide variety of community health-care settings. Among the most frequently selected assignments (as a percentage of total assignments) are these:
- Primary-care physicians in private practice (27.2%)
- Alcoholism- and drug-treatment programs (10.8%)
- Emergency medical care systems (7.5%)
- Indian Health Service hospitals and clinics (including those for Native Alaskans) (6.6%)
- International health assignments (5.6%)
- Nonprimary-care physicians in private practice (5.3%)
- Community health-care centers (3.5%)

• Federal, state, and local public health departments (3.4%)

The Student Role in Selecting and Arranging Field Placements

From its very inception, a hallmark of the program has been to give students an opportunity and a responsibility to identify areas they would like to study. In consultation with faculty advisers, students are expected to take an active role in researching various assignment possibilities and in developing proposals for their field placements. In these proposals, students set forth their learning objectives and plans for how to achieve them.

As an example, one student, who was of Hispanic origin, elected to take an assignment in Minneapolis, Minnesota. Her adviser helped her to identify a community health center that served a largely Hispanic population. In consultation with her adviser, the student developed and subsequently implemented an educational program for diabetic patients.

Students are given written guidelines to assist them in the planning process. In all cases, students must state in writing their objectives and how they plan to achieve them. Each plan must be approved by a student's faculty adviser and field preceptor based upon their assessment of its appropriateness and feasibility.

Whatever the assignment, every student is required to study the health-care system where he or she is assigned. Students are required to make and record observations about (1) the structure, objectives, and financing of the health-care setting; (2) the population served; and (3) the types of health problems that they experience. Both faculty advisers and field preceptors help to orient students to the role of relevant cultural factors.

One of the authors of this paper (Banks) assigns a faculty adviser to work with each medical student. These assignments are made based upon the student's interests and the expertise of the participating faculty member. Periodic faculty meetings are held to review the program and to discuss any problems that may arise.

Additional Academic Requirements

Each student is required to keep a daily log or diary in which he or she records activities, impressions, feelings, etc. The log or diary is reviewed by the faculty adviser and returned to the student. Students must also write reports in which they describe the assigned health-care settings, provide a summary of their activities, and describe any service projects that were completed. The written report is evaluated by the student's faculty adviser. Finally, each student must make an oral presentation at one of the seminar sessions. Students are required to provide in their oral reports brief summaries of their papers. In addition, they are asked to comment upon whether or not their assignments contributed to their personal and professional growth. Participating in these sessions are School of Public Health faculty, medical students, and, sometimes, field preceptors.

Evaluation of the Student's Academic Performance

Each student is evaluated on the basis of the following: (1) the prospectus or proposed study plan; (2) the log of activities or diary; (3) the written report; (4) the oral presentation at the seminar session; and (5) the evaluation of the student's performance by the field preceptor. The evaluation by the field preceptor is especially important. Obviously, the field preceptor has provided daily supervision of the student and is most familiar with the student's activities.

Based on all of the above information, the student's faculty adviser determines what grade shall be assigned. A pass/fail system is employed. However, honors are awarded to students whose performance is superior. Commendations are given to students whose performance is excellent. Letters are sent to each student who receives honors or a commendation. Copies of these letters are placed in the student's College of Medicine files. These letters are referred to in the dean's letter that is sent out as part of a student's residency applications.

Some Cooperating Programs

A program of this scope and magnitude naturally requires the cooperation and assistance of a number of important organizations and programs. These include (1) the Rural Health Committee of the Ohio State Medical Association, (2) the Ohio State University Area Health Education Center, (3) the Office of Primary Care and Rural Health of the Ohio Department of Health, (4) the National Health Service Corps, (5) the Appalachian Regional Commission, (6) the Indian Health Service, and (7) the American Medical Student Association.

Typical Role and Responsibilities of Students

As has been noted, students participate in a rich variety of assignments. Typically, they are actively involved in the clinical care of patients. Sometimes, they also engage in special projects or activities. For example, a student may develop an educational program about sexually transmitted diseases for patients who are served by an inner-city neighborhood health clinic. Or a student may examine chemical exposures of migrant agricultural workers. Whatever the assignment, however, students are expected to study the health-care system where they are assigned. They are expected to learn something about how a particular program is organized and funded, the type of services it provides, and the types of populations it serves. They are also expected to examine the role that cultural factors play in this system.

As an example, one student participated in an assignment in Holmes County, Ohio, an area with a large Amish population. He visited a number of community health agencies. He was also actively involved in patient care at the local community hospital. In both his written and oral reports, the student made insightful comments about the culture of the area and how it impacted health care and health behaviors.

Each student is asked to provide an evaluation of his or her assignment. These evaluations help in assessing the quality of the assignments. Seminar discussions are also useful in this regard.

Preceptors' and Agencies' Perceptions of Student Participants

Preceptors and the agencies where they are employed are typically very positive about working with the medical students. They see student assignments as an opportunity to inform the students about their specialties and the agencies with which they work. Sometimes, long-standing friendships develop between medical students and their preceptors. No financial remuneration has ever been given to a field preceptor or his or her agency. It is noteworthy that some preceptors have been involved in the program since its inception.

Key Ingredients in Sustaining the Field Placement Program

When we began the field placement program in 1971, all medical students at the Ohio State University — approximately 240 each year — were required to participate. In order to accommodate such a large number of students, program staff consisted of a faculty coordinator, five other faculty members (all devoting a small percentage of their time to the program), one full-time administrative assistant, one full-time secretary, and two half-time graduate teaching associates.

In 1979, a major change occurred as the program became elective (a change brought about due to modifications in the clinical curriculum, not dissatisfaction with the program). Now, only about 60 students per year participate. Obviously, this number does not require the extensive staff formerly necessary. One of the authors (Banks) and his secretary are now responsible for coordinating the entire program.

Regardless of program size, an enthusiastic faculty willing to work with medical students remains vitally important. This faculty must meet one-on-one with students and maintain relationships with individuals in a variety of health-care and community agency settings. Another program necessity is an office capable of maintaining information regarding possible student assignments and financial assistance, and able to help with program coordination.

The Community Project

The objectives of the Community Project are to provide each medical student with a better understanding of (1) psychosocial aspects of health care, (2) the relationship between the financing of care and the delivery of care, and (3) the importance of the community context within which health-care services are delivered.

Because of their considerable experience in working with medical students, the authors of this paper were asked to become the codirectors of the Community Project. All first-year medical students at the Ohio State University College of Medicine are required to participate in the project, which is a component of the Medical Humanities and Behavioral Sciences Program.

Each year, letters are mailed to representatives of a number of health agencies in central Ohio to inquire about their willingness to participate in this program. This list of potential agencies is compiled on the basis of past participation and with the addition of new agencies identified by the codirectors.

Representatives of participating agencies are required to orient students to their services. They are also required to assist students in arranging interviews with both agency staff and clients. Finally, representatives evaluate student performance and assess the overall quality of the student assignments.

Students are randomly assigned to one of 80 community agencies in central Ohio. Each student is required to spend a total of 12 hours at a community agency observing how it operates. The student, using a specially prepared study guide, is required to interview both agency personnel and clients. At the conclusion of their assignments, students give oral reports about their experiences in small groups facilitated by faculty members of the College of Medicine.

Students are required to submit evaluation forms in which they assess their assignments. Several years ago, analysis of these forms indicated that a substantial number of students had been disappointed that they were not able to have a more hands-on experience. Many indicated that they actually wanted to provide a service, not just observe. Thus, in the spring of 1994, a survey was conducted to ask students about service and how the College of Medicine might facilitate such involvement. Three themes consistently emerged from this survey. First, responses confirmed that there were a substantial number of students interested in community service. Second, the three main barriers to engaging in service appeared to be (1) lack of time, (2) difficulty in initiating and coordinating service opportunities, and (3) lack of recognition by the medical community of the importance of community service (e.g., recognition that would enhance one's chances in the residency match process). Third, a number of students felt that participation in community service should be an elective rather than a mandatory component of the curriculum.

Building on the results of the survey, we decided to initiate a pilot program called the Community Service Project Option. Under this program, students are given the option of selecting an agency that they would like to work with (rather than being randomly assigned). Students who wish to participate in the service option are required to submit brief statements describing their proposed service activities. If the proposed service projects are affiliated with recognized community health agencies and are judged to be useful by faculty and agency representatives, the codirectors approve them. Although students are required to provide a minimum of 12 hours of service to their host agencies, they typically participate for more than the required minimum. The codirectors are available to assist students in selecting appropriate agencies and in developing proposals.

In 1995, a total of 24 students participated in the Community Service Project Option. They participated in a wide range of service activities at 15 different community agencies. Two students, for example, helped to tutor clients at the local Volunteers of America agency in math and English. Another student engaged in recreational activities and socialized with patients at a nursing home.

From the beginning, participating students and agencies were enthusiastic about the service option and felt that it met important goals. However, some students suggested that it had been difficult to identify suitable community placements. The codirectors then decided to sponsor a community agency fair. A small group of interested faculty and students planned and coordinated this event, and on November 1, 1995, representatives from 29 community agencies participated, meeting informally with students from medicine, allied medicine, and public health to explain the mission of their agencies and to provide information about possible service opportunities. Student attendance exceeded the codirectors' expectations. For example, one agency — Cities in Schools–Columbus — talked to some 60 students.

In 1996, a total of 49 students participated in the Community Service Project Option with 26 community agencies. Evaluations by the students were quite positive. They cited several benefits of participation: First, they felt they were able to gain a deeper understanding of how a health agency works; second, they believed this opportunity enhanced their understanding of psychosocial aspects of illness and health care; third, they reported enhanced feelings of personal efficacy (e.g., feeling like they "made a difference" in someone's life) and a sense of satisfaction with being of service to the community. Based on this feedback as well as feedback from agency representatives, the authors plan to continue to make the Community Service Project Option available to students for the foreseeable future.

Lessons the Authors Have Learned

We have learned much from our roles in these two programs. First, sufficient resources must be available to develop and implement initiatives like these. Enthusiastic and energetic faculty and staff must be willing to work with students. Second, medical students participate enthusiastically in such opportunities. They are especially enthusiastic in those instances in which they have been involved in the selection and formulation of their assignments. Last, staff of health-care centers and community agencies are also enthusiastic about these initiatives. They feel a sense of mission in introducing medical students to their programs and services. They are cognizant that today's medical students are tomorrow's physicians. They also recognize that service-learning activities by medical students contribute positively to their work and mission.

University of Connecticut School of Medicine: An Urban Partnership

by Judy Lewis

The partnership between the University of Connecticut (UConn) and the Hartford community was founded upon several principles: that it should be mutually beneficial; that the community should have a voice in educational policy, course operation, and student evaluation; and that flexibility would be required on both sides. The partnership has evolved and expanded over a period of some 20 years, and many lessons have been learned. This chapter provides an analysis of the experience and lessons that may be generalized to programs in other communities.

Background

Prior to an in-depth discussion of this partnership, it is important to provide some background information on the medical school and the community, as well as some general historical background.

The UConn medical school was one of a group of schools that were developed in the early to middle 1960s. The purpose of these new institutions was to educate primary-care physicians, and they were all considered to be innovative in this respect. However, most schools quickly became quite traditional in their approach to education and educational outcomes. UConn was no exception. As the only public medical school in the state, it sat in the shadow of an important Ivy League institution that trained physicians for national leadership.

UConn began with a nondepartment-/nondiscipline-based orientation to teaching, choosing instead to develop an integrated approach to social science, biological science, and clinical medicine with an emphasis on primary care. However, a departmental approach to teaching quickly gained primacy, especially in the clinical years. Although UConn remained innovative in terms of its organ-system approach to basic science and its strong clinical medicine curriculum beginning in the first semester and continuing throughout the first two years, academic reputations continued to be built on specialization and research, not education and primary care. Soon, the UConn program had a good reputation and resembled most traditional medical schools. Although it did maintain an emphasis on teaching clinical skills, with a focus on the doctor-patient relationship, its graduates were often actively discouraged from careers in primary care.

Most graduates went into subspecialties.

One of the forces favoring nonmainstream interests was that UConn came into existence at a time when there was increasing awareness of the oversupply of hospital beds and regulations to limit further increases where they were not needed. Hartford was an area with too many hospital beds, and the university was limited to building a small academic hospital (235 beds). Hence, it needed to work with community hospitals to provide enough sites for student education. This required development of linkages with the three major local hospitals as well as hospitals in several other nearby communities. These were important clinical training sites and provided the initial contact with residents of urban Hartford. Unfortunately, it was necessary to close the only public hospital in the city to release allocated beds needed to build the academic hospital. This caused many hard feelings about the medical school's reducing access to health services to some of the neediest in the community.

The Community

Hartford is one of the poorest cities in the richest state in the country. It is a city that has a diverse population (one-third African American, one-third Hispanic, one-third white) and many health and social problems. It is the capital of the state, and has a population of 139,000. The contrast between Hartford and the state of Connecticut in terms of population composition is demonstrated in the graph opposite.

While the city of Hartford is relatively small, the metropolitan area is about 800,000. The city is surrounded by affluent suburbs. One example of this very apparent contrast is the comparison of Hartford and one of its adjacent suburbs, West Hartford, as shown below:

	Hartford	West Hartford
median family income	$16,763	$66,724
college education	6.6%	62.9%
manager/professional	15.7%	48.9%
single parent	68.3%	12.0%
receive AFDC	60.0%	1.8%
non-English primary language	50.9%	7.7%

Farmington, where the medical school is located, is quite similar to West Hartford. Many of the clinical experiences the students have are based in Hartford. Therefore, it is critical for students to gain an understanding of this urban population, their living situations, their needs, their strengths, and the resources available to them.

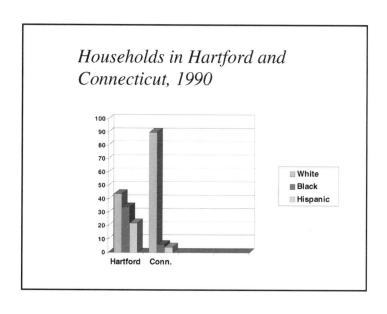

School of Medicine

As previously stated, the relationship between the community and the UConn School of Medicine began rather poorly. With the closure of the public hospital in Hartford, the university hospital was supposed to continue service provision to the urban population. However, there were many barriers that prevented city residents from using the university hospital, including the fact that there was no convenient transportation from Hartford to Farmington. The medical school was viewed by city residents as the "white palace" or "white elephant" on the hill. After this uneasy beginning, efforts began to repair the relationship.

In 1970, during the transition in hospital services from McCook Hospital in Hartford to UConn in Farmington, UConn received an allocation from the state legislature to open the Burgdorf Health Center. This health center was to provide primary care to the residents of the north end of Hartford, who were losing their hospital and its clinics. Pediatric, internal medicine, and obstetrics and gynecology clinics were developed. The Burgdorf Health Center has continued to provide primary-care services to this community. Its administrative structure has changed with the consolidation of health resources in the city, and it is now operated by UConn and the Mt. Sinai/St. Francis hospital consortium. The Burgdorf recently moved into a beautiful new facility across the street from its former site.

In 1978, the first urban Area Health Education Center (AHEC) in the country was funded in Hartford. This was a multidisciplinary program that included the schools of nursing, allied health, and pharmacy from the main university campus in Storrs, as well as medical students from Farmington. The AHEC provided funding for some of the initial linkages with community programs. Several programs, such as the Hartford Visiting Nurse and Home Care Program, the Hartford Dispensary (a methadone maintenance and substance-abuse treatment program), and the Hispanic Health Council, received funding to provide community experiences for students in the health professions schools. This program was funded for seven years. When it ended, many of the community experiences in the other health professions schools also ended.

However, through the primary-care clerkship at the medical school, these experiences were maintained. There was no funding available for any of the community programs once AHEC funding ended. However, this was not necessarily a negative influence. The primary-care clerkship began in academic year 1980-81, and therefore overlapped with the AHEC. This clerkship had a strong community-oriented primary-care emphasis, with 40 percent of its educational time devoted to direct community experience, seminars with a community and clinical focus, and a primary-care project that included a community component. During the period of AHEC funding, some of the community programs were given financial support for their educational activities and some were not; this inequity caused problems in developing community partnerships. When the AHEC ended, it removed the inequity and made it possible to renegotiate with all community programs and make the linkages mutually beneficial. An important lesson was learned: Payment to community programs for their educational services is not necessarily the best exchange or basis for partnership.

From the beginning, community programs were involved in planning the educational goals and activities of the primary-care clerkship. Community representatives sat on the Subject Committee and were invited to curriculum retreats. University faculty and staff made site visits to each program to find out about its services, educational interests, and willingness to participate in program planning. As a result of these activities, goals and objectives were developed, and students were evaluated by the community programs based on their performance in meeting these objectives. This clerkship evolved over time from a required six-week rotation in the fourth year to a required eight-week rotation in the third year. All curriculum changes were made with the active participation of community partners.

Community-Based Education

The Community-Based Education Program was formally begun in 1984, when activities expanded to include a first-semester component of the Introduction to Clinical Medicine (ICM) course. This was a new part of the curriculum designed to teach students about the patient perspective on health and illness, with a focus on chronic illness. Prior to learning any formal medical history, students were matched with patients and families affected by chronic illness and visited them in their homes during the fall semester of the first year. Students averaged six visits during this time. Patients and families were identified through community programs. Students wrote journals about what they had learned during each visit, and discussed their experiences in small groups with clinical and social science faculty. While the idea for this new curriculum component was generated by university faculty, it was based on many discussions with community program representatives. A group of these representatives came together to help shape the goals and objectives as well as what the students needed to know before they began their home visits. In order to learn about available services and the community setting, students began their experience by conferring with the community program that had identified their ICM-A patient. This initiative was very successful; patients and families really appreciated the opportunity to teach students at an early stage in their education. Students learned a great deal about the process and impact of chronic illness, as well as about family, home, and community environments. Community program leaders felt that this experience benefited their patients in many ways. Some of the community program staff served as instructors for the students' small-group discussions. This ICM course continued from 1984 to 1994, when the entire medical school curriculum was revised.

In 1990, a requirement of 15 hours of community service was introduced. This evolved from several primary-care clerkship projects that identified a need to provide health care for the homeless and other underserved populations. Based on these projects, free clinics were established at homeless shelters in Hartford. The clinics were student-run with assistance and guidance from the shelter staff and clinical supervision by volunteer physician faculty. The establishment of these clinics created a discussion about community service in general and the importance of institutional commitment and support for these activities. Malpractice coverage was also identified as an issue. Students were covered by institutional malpractice insurance only if they were engaged in a required educational activity. A student-faculty committee studied the issue of community service and recommended that the 15-hour requirement be accepted as part of the curriculum. This was approved by the School of Medicine Faculty Council and was implemented for the Class of 1994. The requirement provided an incentive for all students to gain some experience in community service. It also ensured malpractice coverage and other institutional support, such as funding for educational materials, for the ongoing activities.

The initial homeless shelter clinics have continued to grow. The first clinic, South Park Inn Medical Clinic, has now been in operation 10 years. It has been equipped entirely through donations and fundraising efforts. The South Park Inn Medical Clinic offers services 6-10 pm two nights a week and provided 1,334 patient visits in 1995-96. It has developed linkages with a nearby community hospital and a community health center for follow-up and referral. This program received the Connecticut Higher Education Community Service Award in 1993. There is also a seven-year-old clinic for children and adolescents at the Salvation Army South Marshall Street Shelter as well as a new clinic, the YMCA Adolescent Girls' Clinic, that provides basic gynecological and primary-care services.

Community service activities have expanded to include many health education projects. One of these is a major initiative in the Hartford public schools. In 1994, the school system eliminated its elementary school health education program. One of the first-year medical students found out about this during an urban health elective and, with the help of several other first-year students, began a community service project. Working closely with one of the health education staff members in the Hartford public schools, they developed a six-session curriculum, focusing on growth, sexuality, and decision making. In 1996, 56 medical and dental students taught in 17 elementary schools. This program has been recognized with an award from the State Department of Higher Education and has been recognized nationally. Other health education projects include information about health professions careers and mentoring of inner-city youth, cardiac rehabilitation, and support for children and families with serious illnesses. Students have the option of participating in an ongoing community service program, developing a new one, or creating their own individual community service activity. The community service requirement was originally overseen by an advisory committee with community, student, and university faculty membership. Once guidelines became operational and the new 1995 curriculum was implemented, this function was assumed by the Community Curriculum Planning Committee.

As noted, the new curriculum began in 1995 and includes four years of community-based education (see chart on page 89). The components of community-based education (CBE) were based on recommendations from community partners, university faculty, and students. Data and experiences from previous community activities were used to generate a template for an integrated curriculum that would build on student skills over time, and in which students could move from observer-learners to learner-contributors. All required community experiences are integrated with clinical education. Overall, the new curriculum was designed to emphasize independent learning, problem solving, and the general skills required of all physicians, including an understanding of population factors and community health. The CBE curriculum was designed by the Community Curriculum Planning Committee, which has representation from community programs, university faculty, and students. This group meets monthly to set policy, oversee and evaluate implementation, and make recommendations for appropriate changes. There are 28 members. Broader community, university faculty, and student input on specific experiences is provided by evaluation forms and workshops/meetings held twice during the year, as well as through continuous communication with CBE program staff.

Major changes in clinical education have involved a shift from inpatient to ambulatory training sites. This occurs in the students' first two years and is accomplished by increasing the time for the Clinical Medicine course from one afternoon to two afternoons per week. Under the new arrangement, one afternoon is devoted to small-group sessions that teach basic clinical skills, such as interviewing, medical history, behavioral change, physical diagnosis, and community health. The other afternoon is spent applying these skills at "Student Continuity Practice" sites. These are internal medicine, family medicine, and pediatric practices in which each student has a physician mentor and develops a relationship with patients. Student responsibility for patient care increases over time. Student Continuity Practice extends into the third year, with small groups meeting less frequently. The third-year curriculum was also dramatically revised to include two courses, an eight-month "Multidisciplinary Ambulatory Experience" and a four-month "Inpatient Experience." In the Multidisciplinary Ambulatory Experience, students spend four to eight weeks in each of the major disciplines (pediatrics, internal medicine, family medicine, obstetrics and gynecology, surgery, and psychiatry) and continue with their Student Continuity Practice one-half day per week. In the fourth year, there are five months of required experience. Three of these months are devoted to the "Acute-Care Experience," which includes a month-long subinternship (in a discipline selected by the student), a month in critical care, and a month in emergency medicine. The other two months are reserved for the "Selective," an in-depth experience in research, education, or health intervention. The community can be the site for any of the focus areas of the Selective.

Community-based education is a component of the major themes of the Clinical Medicine course in each of the first two years. Health promotion and wellness is the organizing theme for the first year of the Clinical Medicine course (this parallels a focus on normal biology and physiology in the first year of basic science studies); illness and disease are the second-year focus (the basic sciences concentrate on pathophysiology as well). Community-based education provides an introduction to communities and community influences on health and illness in the first year. In the Clinical Medicine course, the community-based education curriculum is based in each student's Student Continuity Practice community. Students begin by learning about their Student Continuity Practice, patients, and the community served by the practice. A community orientation is provided through local programs such as health departments and social service providers. Students then identify a community organization with which they would like to work in developing a health promotion/education session. In the spring semester, they visit this program, conduct a needs assessment, develop a teaching plan, and deliver and evaluate the session. Community preceptors provide feedback about the effectiveness of this session. In the second year of the Clinical Medicine course, students go out with a home-care agency serving their Student Continuity Practice community to learn about home care, home health assessment, and chronic illness. In the spring semester, students make home visits to a Student Continuity Practice patient with a chronic illness to learn more about that patient's experiences and to better understand his or her health needs. Because the Student Continuity Practices are located in a variety of communities all over the state of Connecticut, the network of community partners has grown considerably over time and has expanded well beyond the greater Hartford area. Development of the additional community linkages, syllabi and curriculum materials, and the student/community tracking required for the new Clinical Medicine course curriculum was partially supported by a grant from the Health Professions Schools in Service to the Nation Program (HPSISN). The third year of the Clinical Medicine course community curriculum is coordinated with the Multidisciplinary Ambulatory Experiences in the community.

The third-year community-based education curriculum was developed to allow integration with each of the primary-care clinical disciplines. It requires approximately half a day every week, depending on the clinical experience involved. As was described earlier, most of the outpatient clinical experiences are in Hartford. Hence, while the majority of Student Continuity Practice sites are in suburban locations, the third year provides an opportunity for all students to learn about urban minority populations. In pediatrics, the curriculum involves learning about children and child development through day-care centers, schools, and child-protection services, with an emphasis on how physicians work and communicate with these important resources. In obstetrics and gynecology, students learn about the resources available to high-risk pregnant women. These include, in addition to the community-based outreach programs providing home visits and follow-up services, the many services available at their inner-city clinical sites — services such as case management; nutrition, social work, and HIV counseling; substance-abuse treatment; and violence prevention. In medicine, students choose from a list of community programs that includes home care, hospice, rehabilitation, substance-abuse treatment, elder care, health education, and other prevention programs. In family medicine, students are once again placed in a variety of communities around the state so that their community assignment is to learn about the local resources their patients use, accompanying their patients to these services whenever possible. Students often use their community time in family medicine to learn about alternative and complementary treatments such as chiropractic, naturopathy, acupuncture, herbal therapies, etc. Students debrief about their community experiences in small groups at the end of each discipline/rotation. Feedback from the community programs is incorporated into an overall community medicine evaluation for the Multidisciplinary Ambulatory Experience. In addition to these experiences, students in the Multidisciplinary Ambulatory Experience also do a project on a topic of their choosing, which may include examining relevant epidemiology and community resources.

The fourth year of the new curriculum was recently implemented. It is not yet clear how many students will choose to do their Selective requirement in the community. A Selectives booklet was compiled and distributed to third-year students. It lists 124 Selectives project ideas generated from a mailing to university faculty, affiliated hospital faculty, Student Continuity Practice preceptors, and community preceptors. Almost one-third of the listings are from community programs.

Community Partners

Community partners have been involved in planning and evaluating the evolving CBE curriculum since its inception. While committee representation is one method of participation, it is by its nature limiting in the number of programs represented. Efforts to involve broader community partner input have included two events to which all community programs are invited — a fall reception and a spring workshop. In addition, communication is maintained through a bimonthly newsletter, site visits, and telephone conversations. The newsletter has proved to be especially important, and the CBE Office receives many requests for information and student projects as a result of this publication. All new community programs are visited at least once prior to their working with students; existing programs are visited when new staff take responsibility for student precepting — and otherwise when a visit is requested and/or staff time permits. Finally, there are many other opportunities for communication through the various community board activities and local conferences in which CBE staff participate.

Recognition of the contributions of community preceptors has been an important component of the partnership. Community agency staff who work with our students on an ongoing basis are given adjunct faculty appointments in the Department of Community Medicine; those who work with our students for a one-time event, such as a home-care program nurse who takes the student on a home visit, receive a certificate of recognition for each year of participation. These certificates are presented at the annual reception each fall. In the fall of 1997, the 10th annual reception took place, and plaques were presented to those agencies and individuals who had made long-term contributions to community-based education programs. Other sources of recognition/compensation are being explored. The CBE director has been part of a medical school committee that is exploring incentives for community-based faculty. This committee was established because of the Student Continuity Practice initiative, but it is significant that the dean has recognized the importance of providing equivalent incentives for equivalent time to community preceptors as well as clinical preceptors. A teaching unit has been defined, and a reimbursement amount per teaching unit is being established. This amount will be more at the level of a recognition stipend than a reimbursement for time actually spent. However, it can be used by physicians and community preceptors to help support attendance at professional meetings and other discretionary activities.

Evaluation

Another aspect of community preceptors' being recognized as faculty is the part they play in the formal student evaluation process. For one-time or brief student contact experiences, a simple form is used to get feedback from the community on the student and the value of the activity. For example, at the end of the first year, all community preceptors who worked with students on their health education experience are sent a brief survey to solicit their views of the structure of the experience, the role of the student, and the value of the health education presentation. When there is ongoing interaction with a student, such as in the primary-care clerkship or the multidisciplinary ambulatory experience, the community preceptor completes a student performance evaluation that is incorporated into the formal student evaluation for the course. This makes it clear to students, and to university and community faculty, that these preceptors are part of the education team.

Information collected from students, university faculty, and community preceptors has been used to improve communication about the curriculum. It is an important part of feedback, program assessment, and curriculum development efforts. Summaries of the results of this evaluation are provided to community partners through the newsletter and at the fall and spring meetings. These data are used to generate discussion about the strengths and weaknesses of the community experiences and to provide an opportunity for reflection about the philosophy and implementation of the program. This dialogue is an important component of the partnership.

Most important, we have tried to develop a university-community partnership that is mutually beneficial, one in which the community has a voice in educational policy, course operation, and student evaluation. This has worked but has required considerable flexibility and responsiveness to the changing needs of community programs and curricula. When community program staff change, grants are due, or accreditation site visits are scheduled, the university has had to find alternative placements for students. This has resulted in a fairly large range of community programs and keeps community-based education in touch with what is happening at different levels of the community. These circumstances have also required flexibility on the part of students, since at any given point in time, the program they select for placement may not be available. Changes in the overall medical school curriculum have also necessitated changes in the community curriculum. However, because the CBE program philosophy pivots on mutuality and benefits for all partners, the flexibility needed to sustain necessary changes has been forthcoming.

Learning to identify sources of benefit to community partners has also been part of an evolving process. It is important to point out that most community programs participate in health professions educational programs for one major reason: They believe such participation will improve the quality of future doctors and other professionals. This is not necessarily something from which the programs themselves will directly benefit, and their altruism deserves to be recognized and valued in and of itself. In fact, community programs give much more to the students than our students give to them. However, we have tried to identify some "paybacks." These take many different forms: community service activities, health education presentations, a forum for programs to network with one another, student papers and presentations, and, more recently, the Selectives projects in the new curriculum. Community partners recognize that many of their early interactions with students will not result in any direct benefit to their programs or their communities, but that there will be other opportunities that will have this potential. This is an important element of partnership development.

Finally, while students may not be in a particular community long enough to make a substantial contribution, the faculty can forge stronger alliances. In fact, this is critical for program development and partnering. Faculty must be recognized as trusted participants in local community health. In this way, they provide role models for students.

The partnership between the University of Connecticut School of Medicine and the Hartford community has evolved and grown over the years. Mutual respect and collaboration have been the mainstays of this partnership. Challenges will continue to present themselves, but a strong foundation will support creative problem solving and the development of new approaches to this important area of medical education.

Community-Based Education Activities in the UConn School of Medicine Curriculum

Community Education Activity	Minimum Hours	Year 1	Year 2	Year 3	Year 4
Introduction to Community Health	5	CMC			
Health Education	12	CMC			
Home Health Assessment	12		CMC		
Community Resources	8-16 x 4			MAX	
Special Projects	320*				S
Community Service	15	CS	CS	CS	CS

CMC: Clinical Medicine course — community experiences linked to Student Continuity Practice site.

MAX: Multidisciplinary Ambulatory Experience — eight-month block of family medicine, internal medicine, pediatrics, obstetrics and gynecology, surgery, and psychiatry; community agency experiences are integrated in the first four disciplines.

CS: Community service requirement — can occur in any year of the curriculum; the range of hours is from the minimum of 15 to several hundred; most students exceed the minimum requirement.

*S: While the two-month Selective is required, it takes place in the community only by student choice; capstone experience in research, education, or intervention; all three types may be community-based.

Initiating, Maintaining, and Sustaining Community Partnerships:
Developing Community-Based Academic Health Professions Education Systems

by Bruce Bennard, Bruce Behringer, Carol Gentry, Mary Jane Kelley, Paul E. Stanton, Jr., and Wanda Vaghan

In 1996, the James H. Quillen College of Medicine at East Tennessee State University introduced a fifth consecutive cohort of first-year medical students to a three-year multiprofessional curriculum that emphasizes health professions education within a community-oriented service environment. Started with grant funding, the Community Partnership Initiative has been sustained jointly by the involved colleges and communities. This paper examines this successful effort from the perspective of governance and leadership.

The Community Partnership Initiative: An Overview

In 1989, the Colleges of Medicine, Nursing, and Public and Allied Health joined with the two northeast Tennessee rural communities of Mountain City/Johnson County and Rogersville/Hawkins County in a successful effort to obtain a Community Partnership Initiative grant from the W.K. Kellogg Foundation. One goal of the grant was to shift substantial portions of health professions education from traditional academic centers dependent upon large hospitals and campus classrooms to rural community-academic systems developed by the communities and the university. A second major goal was to create a multiprofessional curriculum that accommodated the needs of the three colleges in the university's Division of Health Sciences. This paper focuses primarily upon the first goal (academy-community partnership) but also references the second because the two are intertwined. Indeed, "thinking in terms of single innovations is inherently limiting, [when] . . . we are in reality faced with attempting to cope with multiple innovations" (Fullan and Stiegelbauer 1991).

Medical students first entered the program in Mountain City in 1992, while Rogersville accepted them a year later. At East Tennessee State, medical students are offered a three-year curriculum that includes a four-month rural, primary-care clerkship in their third year. In all, they receive approximately 25 percent of their education in one of the counties. As a result, they become familiar with the community at large, the existing health system, and the multiple roles of the community practitioner. Their understanding of the community is enhanced by taking courses designed in part by community curriculum committees, by learning from community practitioners and patients, and by engaging in service. All this reinforces their interest in practicing in a medically underserved area.

The three years that medical students spend in the community also help sustain community interest in the program. Community members value students who stay and serve the community as their professional competence grows. One board member explained that her willingness to commit time to the program was reinforced by the recognition that one of the students had become instrumental in the care of her ailing mother for a period extending over two years. She explained, "I willingly serve the program because it is good for the community, but the family benefit adds to the commitment." Community leaders also acquire a depth of understanding about medical education that makes them as interested in the quality of the community-based curriculum and its impact upon student performance as they are in improvements in community health services.

Initiating, Maintaining, and Sustaining the Program: Principles and Practice

The story of how the community partnership program was initiated, maintained, and sustained can be understood as a continuum in which distinctive principles and practices were exercised. First, they were established to start the program; then they were extended, increasing the likelihood of successful program implementation and sustaining the newly formed community-academic health systems. These principles and practices can be effectively introduced in four broad statements.

• **The leadership in the health professions colleges became directly involved in medically underserved communities. This involvement was never directive; it addressed a community-identified need and occurred prior to the Community Partnership Initiative.** In Mountain City, community leaders concerned with the deterioration of health services due to the closing of the community hospital (subsequently reopened in 1992) and a concomitant 75 percent reduction in the number of physicians within the county sought help from the Division of Health Sciences. The rapid response of the deans led to the establishment of clinical facilities provided by the Department of Family Medicine and the College of Nursing. The extended-hours clinic staffed by nurse practitioners provided care in the evening and on weekends, and the family practice clinic attracted two new physicians to the community. The clinics also established educational sites for students and residents, thus providing the beginnings of an infrastructure for the Community Partnership Initiative. While these developments did not employ a formal academy-community planning structure, the active, sustained involvement of the deans and some of the department chairs demonstrated accessibility, interest, and responsiveness to community leaders, who in turn exhibited willingness to support health professions education programs with which they had almost no familiarity.

The situation in Rogersville paralleled, albeit less dramatically, that which existed in Mountain City. The county hospital patient census was low, and there was a growing shortage of physicians. The leadership in Rogersville turned to the university's Division of Health Sciences for assistance. The deans became involved in developing solutions, thus leading to community support for the initiative.

Direct community involvement by academic leaders continued throughout the grant and postgrant periods. A close working relationship between the Division of Health Sciences and community leaders developed in three distinct ways. First, it was provided for and routinized through program governance (described in subsequent sections of this paper). Second, it occurred via ad hoc activities undertaken as part of program implementation. Third, it was reinforced through participation in foundation-sponsored activities. Some ad hoc activities were ceremonial and offered high-profile opportunities for the university leadership to extend its direct involvement in the community. These included the ceremonies marking the opening of clinical and classroom facilities and community-conducted welcoming and graduation ceremonies for students. As both communities involved in the initiative are distant from campus, the presence of the deans, department chairs, and faculty in community ceremonies illustrated their commitment.

Other ad hoc activities were programmatic in nature. In 1992, concurrent with curriculum development, the program director organized and brokered three focus groups of Johnson County community leaders and health services representatives that examined the type of health-care system best suited for the communities. What emerged was a vision, new to the community, of a system that emphasized both prevention and treatment services.

It is important to note the role that the W.K. Kellogg Foundation played in reinforcing the collaboration between academic and community leaders. It sponsored a series of network meetings that examined leadership, curriculum, community-academic collaboration, and health policy for representatives of the seven community partnership initiatives it funded. The foundation often insisted that both academic and community leaders attend the meetings. Those attending from East Tennessee believe the greatest value of these meetings was the opportunity they provided for leaving the familiar work environment to focus on program issues. Meservey and Richards point out in their chapter in *Building Partnerships* (1996) that providing community and academic leaders opportunities to network with colleagues from other programs contributes to the realization of effective academy-community partnerships. An equally important strategy is providing time for these leaders to discuss issues and to work as a team in an environment outside their daily work routine.

• **The academic leaders committed proactively and publicly to the Community Partnership concept and addressed concerns within the respective schools as articulated by faculty.** During the first years of the initiative, academic leaders continually espoused its importance as it related to the mission of the university and its involved colleges. This countered concerns expressed by some chairs and faculty over loss of control over portions of the curriculum (and presumably a concomitant reduction in its quality). The leaders also supported the program due to their belief that the program represented the "right" approach to professional and publicly supported education within southern Appalachia. They declared that the initiative permitted them to position their colleges for responding to the needs of the emerging health-care system.

While faculty resistance to the initiative exists to this day, it cannot be characterized as severe. However, in early 1992, the level of faculty support was not known. Resistance was not great, but neither was enthusiasm. Conflicts between medicine and nursing faculty regarding interpretation of program objectives made it difficult to develop the curriculum. During a retreat led by the vice president for health affairs, the seriousness of the differences between the two schools was realized, and steps were taken to overcome them. It was also apparent, however, that support for the academy-community partnership concept was adequate. The main concern in medicine was that patient volume for clinical teaching in small community practices might prove inadequate to maintain the quality of clinical education. Once the concerns of the "conventionally minded" faculty were identified, it became possible to maintain adequate faculty support for the program. Using matched control groups and evaluations from clinical rotations, it was demonstrated that students within the initiative acquired clinical skills equivalent to those attained by traditional curriculum students. In-depth interviews of students provided additional data that assured faculty that the clinical experiences provided in the initiative were more than adequate.

The commitment of community leadership to the initiative and its determination to be responsive to faculty concerns have been constants. College of Medicine faculty are kept informed of program progress at monthly faculty meetings. When the initiative neared the end of full grant funding, however, many faculty questioned whether it would be sustained. The executive program director and the deans organized a comprehensive review of the initiative that emphasized its achievements and their support for it in the postgrant period. It was presented to faculty in a forum that involved community representatives and students who emphasized the value of the partnership in both communities. Because the deans sponsored the forum, faculty were aware, whether or not they chose to attend, that they were being provided an opportunity to discuss the future of the initiative.

This continual leadership support has been effective. The 1996 self-study of the College of Medicine that preceded a scheduled Liaison Committee on Medical Education site visit identified the Community Partnership Initiative as contributing to the strengths of the college. During a two-day faculty meeting conducted to review the self-study reports, the dean gave a state of the College of Medicine address in which he identified some of these contributions: First, the program enhanced the working relationship between the College of Medicine and the other colleges in the Division of Health Sciences. Second, it was a mechanism for educational innovations. Third, it brought medical education into rural communities; and fourth, it helped define the medical school's mission and made it visible across the country.

• **Community leaders assumed significant roles in governing the Community Partnership Initiative. This permitted them to be involved in hiring the program director and key faculty, in developing teaching sites, and in implementing courses.** The W.K. Kellogg Foundation insisted upon meaningful community involvement in the governance of the Community Partnership Initiative. The academic leadership supported this view. Community leaders enjoy majority membership on the governing board and the two community advisory boards. The governing board oversees policy and broad implementation issues, including final approval of the annual budget and the hiring of key personnel. The advisory boards support the program within each partnership community. They ensure that the initiative functions smoothly (or nearly so) within the community setting. Each advisory board has committees for student orientation, student housing, and development of community-based teaching resources. Board members individually or collectively help solve problems and avoid crises. For example, in Mountain City, advisory board members helped find a meeting place for students when the teaching site under construction was not ready for the first group of students. The advisory boards consistently have met the challenges of implementing new programs.

Action taken by the governing and advisory boards has secured the interests of the communities and has raised the profile of community leaders within the university. Their involvement in the hiring of the program director and the academic faculty for staffing the community-based academic sites propelled them into an area that has long been a preserve of deans and department chairs. It led to the hiring of an executive director who was the president-elect of the National Rural Health Association and whose strongest credentials were in community health systems. A clear priority of his has been to actualize the partnership concept. He is acknowledged by those in the initiative as the one individual who reinforces the partnership on a day-to-day basis.

The governing and advisory boards sought to hire faculty who would live in the participating communities. This effort has been partially successful. Several full-time academic faculty reside in the communities. The significance of having faculty living on-site is considerable. They establish more effective links between the community and university. Most attend advisory board meetings and are considered by community leaders to be community assets. They have also helped raise community understanding of health professions education. Perhaps most important, the presence of faculty reassures community leaders that the university's commitment to the partnership is long-term.

The governing and advisory boards are mechanisms that have permitted community leaders to assume important roles within the initiative. Their willingness to serve the program and their success in doing so have made community board members spokespersons for the initiative before academic as well as community audiences. They have spoken to the health professions faculty at large about the need and "correctness" of continuing the program when that issue arose, and they gave major presentations on campus for a Kellogg Foundation–coordinated national health-care policy discussion.

• Program leaders committed themselves to a self-education process in order to better understand the two cultures — academic and small rural community — represented in the partnership, particularly pertaining to needs, expectations, and rewards. While leaders on both sides had worked with one another prior to the initiative, the development of a community-based academic system represented a degree of collaboration not previously realized. They soon identified a need for two types of "self-education." One was for academic and community leaders to develop a better understanding of each other's culture. The second type was learning to work effectively as a single entity.

The education of community leaders about health professions education probably represented the most extensive "self-education" engaged in by the governing boards. Many early meetings were utilized, in part, as "seminars" for community leaders to learn about critical elements and phases of medical education, such as the basic sciences, Step One and Two Board Examinations, clerkship rotations, and the "match." They learned how health professions curricula were constructed and about the associated approval process. In this way, community members assimilated the objective of establishing a high-quality curriculum within the community, rather than viewing such an objective as important only to their academic colleagues. Indeed, community commitment to the curriculum led to an important lesson for academic leaders. As part of the plan to sustain the program without foundation support, the deans were inclined to drastically reduce the curriculum's one-week community orientation course to stay inside a shrinking budget. Community leaders demanded that the course be retained. They correctly pointed out that the course was instrumental in introducing students to the community learning environment and that students who had completed the course considered it vital. Their opinion prevailed. The academic leaders learned that the institutional culture can be shortsighted, and that a course that connects students to the community is of equal importance to courses that are more obviously linked to professional credentials.

The second type of self-education was learning how to work together as a team. This was accomplished largely through the actions of the executive program director, who emphasized the process of decision making. Some board meetings were not only seminars but highly interactive "workshops" in which small-group exercises were utilized to enable participants to discuss or brainstorm ideas intended to strengthen the program. Periodically, "process" exercises were used to determine needs and expectations as related to the program. A good example of this occurred in 1994, when the Hawkins County Advisory Board considered what the community "gives to" and "gets from" the initiative. Through brainstorming followed by discussion, the board determined that community contributions included material and nonmaterial support, classroom and clinic sites, an extensive real-world learning environment, citizenry eager to contribute to student learning, an orientation course essential to the curriculum, active participation in program development, and good faith in developing a more mature relationship with East Tennessee State University. The board also believed it contributed to the growing national recognition of the university as a leader in health professions education. In return for such contributions, the board believed the community received priority status from the university for local students wishing to enter health professions education programs, benefits from special curriculum projects such as management of teenage pregnancies, improved health-related data collection, increased stability in the local hospital, valuable experience in educational program development, deeper appreciation for the complexity of health professions education, more reliable information about the university, and an increase in the number of local health providers.

The Johnson County Advisory Board also identified a set of contributions and benefits. Most resembled those identified in Hawkins County, but some were unique. For example, board members believed that community participation had resulted in a degree of collaboration among local political and health interests almost nonexistent prior to the program. The construction of the Johnson County Academic Health Center and a subsequent leasing arrangement with the university required the city and county governments to collaborate in a joint venture for the first time. It also led them to consider the need for a long-term plan for human services.

The exercise was repeated at governing board meetings where university contributions and rewards were also brainstormed. Contributions included allocation of resources, shared power over the curriculum, and sustained expenditure of time by academic leaders. Benefits included a willingness to innovate, new clinical teaching resources, enhanced student and faculty recruitment, program articulation with institutional mission statements, and improved positioning for meeting challenges posed by the emerging health-care system.

Expending time to identify contributions and rewards reinforced the realization by both the community and academic leaders that the contributions of each group were unique and important, and satisfied them that service and educational needs can be linked.

Challenges of Developing Community Partnerships and Lessons Learned

The Community Partnership Initiative can be considered successful. This is the assessment of the College of Medicine, the participating communities, and the Kellogg Foundation. The communities have not "burned out," which is a phenomenon described by one of the foundation's medical education advisers, whose experience with community-based education is extensive. We believe this is due to the collaboration between the communities and the participating colleges and the presence of a tangible academic health professions education system, including university health facilities, within the communities. This demonstrated a sense of permanence. Communities want to educate "their" students rather than students who come and go.

There are other, objective reasons the program can be considered successful. The major goal of creating a community-academy system and a curriculum that reinforced health professions students' interest in rural health care was realized in the first three years. Besides effective governance, the system can boast academic teaching centers in each community, a multi-professional faculty, and numerous clinics and health agency sites suitable for teaching students. The curriculum has proved effective. Medical student graduates of the program have entered primary-care residencies at rates higher than the prevailing high rate for the medical college. The program's medical students perform as well as their counterparts in the traditional program in the basic sciences, on high-stakes national examinations, and in nonprimary-care clerkships. Their clinical skills are also equivalent to those of other medical students, thus demonstrating that extensive hospital exposure is not the only approach to adequately developing clinical skills. Most important, students report value-added benefits associated with the program. Two frequently mentioned are increased levels of professional responsibility due to the absence of resident teams in community hospitals and clinics, and an appreciation for patients as community members rather than as cases briefly encountered in an impersonal clinic or hospital environment.

However, program success has not been easily achieved. Disappointments and difficulties created challenges for the leadership. These difficulties, as well as significant successes, can be discussed in the form of lessons learned.

• **Information about the program needs to be shared equally with community leaders and academic leaders.** During the partnership, community leaders occasionally expressed distress at being uninformed about specifics of program implementation. This distress occurred, in part, because faculty involved on a day-to-day basis with the program were more likely to inform academic leaders than community leaders about elements of student discontent with the curriculum or the community. For their part, the academic leaders did not always share this information with community leaders. They did not want to burden the community with "academic" problems, and they wanted to protect the community from occasional criticism. Although it may be well-intentioned, withholding information of interest to community members limits the partnership. Once academic leaders realize that community leaders are interested in and responsive to program-related problems, even those critical of the community role, the partnership will mature.

• **Involvement of three colleges in the academy-community partnership adds to its complexity, but the advantages outweigh the disadvantages.** Developing a health professions curriculum for the Community Partnership Initiative resulted in leaders from medicine, nursing, and public and allied health working together on a sustained basis. Significant conflict arose between medicine and nursing over basic assumptions, such as the meaning of collaboration. Community leaders were affected by this conflict. At best it was awkward; at worst it made them question the long-term prospects of the program. However, unquestionably, the involvement of the three schools has strengthened implementation of the initiative. Over time, the disputes between medicine and nursing became attenuated, a residual benefit of which was increased community sophistication regarding health professions education. More important, academic leaders never disagreed over the importance of developing community-academy health centers, and each college committed resources toward their realization. Thus, development of the initiative proceeded on a broad front. Also in practice, the deans, on occasion, could share the responsibility for attending meetings in the community, which permitted them to sustain their direct involvement without unduly compromising other administrative responsibilities.

• **Level the playing field as far as possible for all partners in the initiative.** Providing community leaders with majority membership on governing boards and hiring a community-oriented program director helped offset distinct advantages enjoyed by the academic leaders (such as administration of the budget). These decisions still appear sound. In their study of leadership and management in the seven Kellogg Foundation–funded Community Partnership Initiatives, Starnaman and her colleagues (1995) reported:

> Compared to sites at which the boards have a majority of clinical and academic representatives, at sites with majority community representation, participants . . . are more apt to report: greater role clarity and less role conflict; a greater degree of information sharing [that is] clear . . . timely and relevant; a strong sense of shared vision; established ways to handle conflict . . . a sense of shared leadership; more discussion and negotiation . . . and a greater degree of satisfaction and commitment.

• **Academic leaders must be tenacious in communicating their vision for the program and must stay involved in the program, at least until sustainability is realized.** They must communicate their sense of commitment loudly and frequently. Resistance by faculty will exist, along with inertia and complacence. Leaders must be prepared to spend extensive time promoting and defending the program within the walls of academe. Happily, this should become less necessary as the program matures.

• Finally, the most important lesson one can take from this experience is **the importance of listening to community leaders experienced in working with academic partners.** Their message will be simple, direct, and challenging. However stated, it will reinforce the importance of building trust, showing respect, sharing information, and recognizing commitment.

References

Fullan, M.G., and S. Stiegelbauer. (1991). *The New Meaning of Educational Change.* New York, NY: Teachers College Press.

Meservey, P.M., and R.W. Richards. (1996). "Creating New Organizational Structures." In *Building Partnerships: Educating Health Professionals for the Communities They Serve,* edited by R.W. Richards. San Francisco, CA: Jossey-Bass.

Starnaman, S., C. Bland, H. Perlstadt, L. Hernbroff, and R. Henry. (1995). "Building the Partnership Through Leadership and Management Investment in the Future." Paper presented at the W.K. Kellogg Foundation Conference, Building Partnerships: An Agenda for Health Around the World.

Integrating Teaching, Research, and Service at East Tennessee State University:
Action and Accountability in Communities

by Joellen B. Edwards, Joy E. Wachs, Sheila M. Virgin, Bruce A. Goodrow, and James E. Florence

Community-based education for the health professions requires a commitment on the part of academic faculty, students, and community leaders to meet the perceived and actual health and societal needs of participating communities. The academy's requirement of continuing scholarly productivity as a marker of faculty success, the learning needs of students, and the intense and highly visible needs of poor and rural communities for health services are often in competition for a professor's time. This paper describes the results of an effort by faculty from the colleges of Medicine, Nursing, and Public Health, together with the W.K. Kellogg Foundation's Community Partnership Initiative at East Tennessee State University, to create synergy rather than antagonism among these usually conflicting demands on faculty time.

The Problem

All university faculty face conflicting demands in their professional lives for the distribution of their time. Teaching responsibilities must be balanced with the furtherance of new knowledge in their discipline through research efforts. Most universities profess that students come first and that teaching is their most important mission. However, promotions, tenure, and tangible rewards in the system such as raises, office space, funds for travel, and public recognition often stem from the results of research rather than teaching skill and expertise (Boyer 1987). These conflicting demands occur in every discipline within the university. For faculty in health professions education, another demand surfaces: that of the requirement to remain current as a practicing professional and to provide hands-on services in addition to fulfilling scholarly and teaching responsibilities. Practicing health professionals are accountable to society in a way that few other disciplines experience so directly.

More layers of difficulty emerge for faculty involved in the continuing development of health professions education to make it more relevant to the basic health needs of people (Richards 1995). Nearly all reward systems within the health professions disciplines are focused on the promotion of basic research or research within narrow and acutely focused specialty areas. The federal grant system places emphasis on discipline-specific research in the treatment of disease rather than on health promotion and illness prevention across professional groups. Even institutional funding tends to favor narrowly defined research topics. On the other hand, health professions educators who engage in interdisciplinary, community-based teaching and practice must respond not only to the research demands of the university system and the educational needs of students but also to the immense health needs of the populations they serve. Thus, their time commitment to and emotional investment in community problem solving divert them from what the university values most: research results, publication of manuscripts, and procurement of research funding.

The Setting

East Tennessee State University is a comprehensive regional institution serving nearly 12,000 students in undergraduate through doctoral programs. The university is located in northeast Tennessee in the beautiful Blue Ridge section of the Appalachian Mountains. The institution is highly driven by its mission to "serve the region" through business, education, government, health-care systems, and community. The Division of Health Sciences of East Tennessee State University consists of the College of Medicine, the College of Nursing, and the College of Public and Allied Health. The mission of the division is to prepare health professionals in medicine, nursing, public health, and a wide variety of allied health disciplines for primary-care practice. Particular emphasis is placed on the preparation of professionals committed to practice in rural and underserved areas. Like the institution as a whole, the Division of Health Sciences believes in this mission and has achieved significant success in this area. Sixty percent of graduating physicians choose a primary-care residency, and 60 percent of advanced practice nursing graduates elect to practice in health professions shortage areas.

The vision of the university, and within it the vision of the Division of Health Sciences, fosters a climate that stresses connection with constituent communities rather than distance. Over time, and with the excitement and positive outcomes meaningful interaction at the community level brings, partnership has become our standard. This commitment to partnership has fostered a very real integration of the university with the region. Although the words describing promotion and tenure policies have not changed, over time they have been interpreted to increasingly value the service and the scholarly work that emanate from meeting the very real needs of communities.

The Community-Based Project

In 1991, the Division of Health Sciences was awarded a W.K. Kellogg Foundation grant for a Community Partnership Initiative for health professions education. The purpose of this grant was to create an interdisciplinary community-based health professions education program that would focus on the primary-care needs of the local population (see the essay by Bennard et al. elsewhere in this volume). Equal partners in this effort were two rural communities in northeast Tennessee, in Johnson County and Hawkins County, each located approximately one hour from the main campus. The partner communities are federally designated as health professions shortage areas. Socioeconomic status and educational levels are low, while regional rates of chronic illness are high (Tennessee Department of Health 1995).

University faculty from each discipline within the Division of Health Sciences live, teach, practice, and conduct research in rural communities. While most have moved to these communities from outside the area, a few are professionals who grew up in local communities and have returned home. These faculty in particular face the conflicting demands of competing for success in the academic world while meeting the needs of students and providing the services so urgently needed in their home communities. In an effort to consolidate energy and time as they pursue professional careers, faculty have created, in partnership with community members, projects that integrate teaching, research, and service in a way that satisfies the complex demands made upon them.

Strategies for Success

All projects reflect a model of comprehensive, community-based, interdisciplinary primary care (Pullen, Edwards, Lenz, and Alley 1994) that provides the essential framework for success in integrating teaching, research, and service in community-based settings. Its basic tenets include:

1. adaptability to the unique and collective concerns of the community;
2. ability to address the needs of the community for basic primary and preventive care and to provide an entrance into the system for all types of health-care services;
3. opportunities to address comprehensive and holistic community needs;
4. partnership and equality among the professional disciplines and community members.

The first step in utilizing this model calls for interdisciplinary and community collaboration in the assessment of the target population's health and related societal needs. Such assessment can be formally planned, organized, and conducted from an academic perspective, as in the case of the Johnson County health survey (Burkett and Beck 1990, 1993). In other circumstances, a community event can mobilize action, as in the case of the rural traffic fatality study (Goodrow and Virgin 1995). However, regardless of what triggers the assessment, the result is a collaborative team of health professionals and community members who come together to gather data about community concerns. Assessment methodologies vary as appropriate to each situation.

The second step in the process involves the analysis of the data gathered and, from this analysis, formulation of a "diagnosis" of the problem. Faculty, students, and community members agree on the issue to be addressed, as in a study of cardiovascular risk factors (Virgin, Goodrow, and Olive 1995) and school nutrition (Virgin and Wachs 1995). Both strengths and weaknesses are analyzed so that all parties can see the potential as well as the needs of the communities involved.

Step three calls for identification of the interventions to be implemented. These may be primary (Edwards, Lenz, and East 1993), secondary (Ramsey and Glenn 1995), or tertiary interventions that are carried out by teams of faculty, students, and community members. Faculty practice, faculty or community health professionals' mentoring of students, health screenings and educational efforts, and student involvement in community organizations are all examples of intervention strategies aimed at improving the community's health through education, service, and research efforts.

The fourth step requires evaluation of project outcomes. Pre- and postintervention measurements, attitudinal surveys, longitudinal studies, and comparison of epidemiological data are examples of evaluation methodologies that provide the quantitative and qualitative database for scholarly publications, presentations, and grant writing as well as evaluation of student performance and the effectiveness of an intervention in improving the health of community members. At an institution where service and the scholarly work associated with it are valued, students learn through practice in communities, while faculty fulfill their multifaceted roles in teaching, research, and service.

The vignettes presented at the end of this chapter summarize a few of the integrated outcomes that have resulted from the East Tennessee project. Each story references a description of an integrated project, student learning activities, community benefits, and research conducted in conjunction with educational and service endeavors. Student and faculty projects with real community impact, scholarly publications, and formative learning experiences for health professions students testify to the success of the approach here described.

Practical Lessons Learned

Over the years, faculty, students, and community members have learned many lessons in the course of implementing interdisciplinary health professions education designed to meet the needs of the community. Some of these include:

1. Personal relationships developed over time significantly affect the possibility of providing services and educational experiences that are relevant and meaningful to community members. Trust, positive interactions, acceptance of cultural norms, and consistency in joining in the spirit and work of the community are critical to success.

2. Community members need to be included in every possible aspect of teaching, research, and guidance of service delivery. For a project to succeed, community members must "own" their fair share of it — from analysis of need to the reporting of data.

3. Faculty must serve as role models in interdisciplinary and community collaboration. Students learn what they see lived before them and are very critical of lapses in cooperation and respect among team members.

4. Every project must be considered from the perspective of an integrated linking of time and energy. What will students learn from the project? How will this fit into the university's service mission in the community? What data do faculty need to collect to report this effort in the professional literature? These are all key questions that will help generate and focus creative energy.

5. Creative efforts to serve communities require broadly based support. In order to succeed in winning promotion and tenure, as well as in other university reward systems, colleagues and administrators must value the contribution of integrated projects and collaborative efforts. Sufficient attention and public recognition focused on accomplishments in communities help create within the academic community a climate favorable to an integrated, nontraditional approach to teaching, research, and service.

Summary

As faculty, students, and community members implement projects that meet community needs, students gain hands-on, real-world experience relevant to various aspects of health professions education. They learn clinical skills, leadership, community development and organizing, research and evaluation techniques, communication strategies, and the meaning of accountability. They learn to value interdisciplinarity and community collaboration in achieving goals no single discipline or group could achieve alone. They experience what it means to be a health professional in a rural area and how to make a professional presentation. Persistence, flexibility, skill in maneuvering through the complex health-care system, and much, much more become important parts of the curriculum. Community members gain self-confidence, pride in their efforts, and a voice in the preparation of health professions students who will serve their long-term needs. Faculty gain the opportunity to consolidate their teaching, research, and service efforts in a way that is still rare in the university system. They have an opportunity to be part of a community solution rather than observers in an ivory tower. At the same time, they can create research studies that will over the long term provide a basis for federal or foundation funding.

Today we are engaged in changing the culture of health professions education institutions and that of communities as well (Richards 1995). Cultural change takes time, energy, commitment, and persistence. However, this significant investment will bring about new opportunities for improving the health status of community members and the quality of health professionals prepared to practice in those communities. In the long term, this prospect is worth every human and material resource we invest.

References

Beck, R., C. Jijon, and J. Edwards. (1995). "The Relationships Among Gender, Perceived Financial Barriers to Care, and Health Status in a Rural Population." Accepted for publication in *Journal of Rural Health*.

Boyer, E. (1987). *College: The Undergraduate Experience in America*. New York, NY: Harper and Row Publishers.

Burkett, G., and R. Beck. (1990; 1993). "The Johnson County Health Survey." Johnson City, TN: East Tennessee State University.

Edwards, J., C. Lenz, and J. East. (1993). "Nurse-Managed Primary Care: Serving a Rural Appalachian Population." *Family/Community Health* 16(2): 50-56.

Goodrow, B., and S. Virgin. (1995). "Rural Traffic Fatality Study." Johnson City, TN: East Tennessee State University.

Pullen, C., J. Edwards, C. Lenz, and N. Alley. (1994). "A Comprehensive Primary Health Care Delivery Model." *Journal of Professional Nursing* 10(4): 201-208.

Ramsey, P., and L. Glenn. (1995). "Universal Precautions, Compliance, and Exposure Frequency to Patient Body Fluids in Nurses Employed by Urban and Rural Health Care Agencies." *Journal of Rural Health* 11(3): 158-168.

Richards, R., ed. (1995). *Building Partnerships: Educating Health Professionals for the Communities They Serve*. San Francisco, CA: Jossey-Bass.

Tennessee Department of Health. (1995). *Tennessee's Health: Picture of the Present*. Part 2. Nashville, TN: Tennessee Dept. of Health.

Virgin, S., B. Goodrow, and K. Olive. (1995). "Cardiovascular Risk Factors: Identification and Intervention Across the Life Span." Johnson City, TN: East Tennessee State University.

Virgin, S., and J. Wachs. (1995). "School Nutrition Project." Johnson City, TN: East Tennessee State University.

Wachs, J., J. Florence, and S. Virgin. (1995). "Identification and Reduction of Health Risks Among Employees in a Rural County." Johnson City, TN: East Tennessee State University.

Cardiovascular Risk Factors:
Identification and Intervention Across the Life Span

Project Description

A comprehensive community assessment revealed that Hawkins County, Tennessee, had an incidence of cardiovascular disease two to three times higher than the national average. When community members, including county officials, health-care providers, and citizens were asked about their health concerns, "heart problems" were most frequently identified. A team of nursing, medical, and public health students and faculty and community members developed an intervention program aimed to identify cardiovascular risk factors in the county population and educate residents about prevention of heart problems.

Student Learning Activities

The students, mentored by their faculty members, learned to organize and carry out a community assessment using epidemiologic data and personal interviews with community members. They analyzed the quantitative and qualitative data. The students then presented results to community members. In the next phase of the project, identification of specific cardiovascular risk factors, students carried out risk assessments in various settings throughout the county. Once again, students analyzed the data and, based upon the results selected a group of citizens with whom to implement a cardiovascular risk-reduction program. This program is being implemented now. Students have gained experience in the research process, learning how to manage large data sets, time management, assertiveness, leadership skills, specific content related to cardiovascular risk factors and reduction of risk, interdisciplinary collaboration, how to involve the community, and health teaching.

Community Benefits

Community members from all segments of the population were involved in naming their own health concerns and gave direction to the faculty and students as to the main health concern to be addressed. They took pride in contributing to the students' education, and many gained new insight into the possibility of more control over their own health status. The long-term result will be better cardiovascular health in the community.

Research Outcomes

Baseline data on the status of the community's health has been gathered. Preintervention data was gathered on knowledge of risk factors and health risk status for the group selected for specific prevention programs; at the completion of the program, postintervention data on the same measures will be collected. The baseline data will be used for comparison purposes in this study and in many more in the future. Data from the intervention study will be submitted for presentation and publication in a professional journal (Virgin, Goodrow, and Olive 1995).

Rural Traffic Fatality Study

Project Description

This project was the result of a sad but authentic "teachable moment" in a small rural community. A very tragic automobile accident on a narrow country road resulted in the death of three teenagers. In an effort to support community members and to prevent further fatalities, interdisciplinary faculty and students set out to explore issues around the accident.

Student Learning Activities

Under faculty direction, students from medicine, nursing, and public health used epidemiological methods to investigate automobile accidents in the county over a 10-year time period. They discovered that during the previous decade, 13 deaths and 107 injuries had occurred in the same 12-mile stretch of rural, two-lane road. Students contacted the local rescue squad and law enforcement officials with this information. Both groups were surprised and distressed to learn of the clustered pattern of injuries and fatalities on this section of highway. A plan for coordinated community action was developed jointly among students, faculty, and local leaders. A task force consisting of representatives from the school, health-care providers, the rescue squad, law enforcement, political leaders, and students was formed. Further data gathered from accident reports and interviews with accident victims from this area resulted in a plan for increased auto safety that included education, enforcement, and reengineering of severe curves on the road. New driver education curricula for the school were developed, a seat-belt survey was administered by police officers to raise awareness of this important safety factor, and the county altered the angles of several curves. Students learned epidemiological research methods, public relations, small-group leadership, specific content related to auto safety and prevention of accidents, and the importance of community involvement, and they developed skill in community organization around a health and safety issue.

Community Benefits

Community leaders were involved in every step of this learning process. A sense of teamwork and solidarity evolved around this issue. Community members were able to bring about changes that will reduce automobile deaths in the county, and felt empowered to take collective action for the common good.

Research Outcomes

The research outcome from this project was related to the students. Data from the study were used to develop a poster presentation by the student team. Two students were invited to display this poster at a national meeting, thus gaining experience not only in conducting and using research but also in managing a professional presentation at the national level (Goodrow and Virgin 1995).

The Johnson County Health Survey

Project Description

At the beginning of involvement by the Division of Health Sciences in a rural county in the mountains of Tennessee, an interdisciplinary team of faculty, students, and community members initiated a comprehensive survey of various aspects of the community's health. Examples of the areas surveyed included family composition, socioeconomic status, perception of health, accessibility of health-care providers, patterns of use of the health-care system, types of health insurance coverage, health beliefs, types of illnesses and disabilities, community concerns, and many more. A random sample of 243 families was selected using addresses obtained from the local electric company. Initial face-to-face interviews were conducted in the summer of 1990. To obtain a longitudinal view of the changes in health care and health status as faculty and students worked in the community, the same residents were interviewed in 1991 and 1993 as well.

Student Learning Activities

Students and faculty from nursing, medicine, and public health were trained as data collectors and conducted the face-to-face interviews during each data-collection cycle. Students participated in the refinement of interview questions for the second and third interview schedules, in data entry, and in analysis. Data from the survey have been used to engage the students in many health-promotion, illness-prevention, and clinical-care activities over the years. Examples include the development of primary-care services, a program in conjunction with the public health department to increase the proportion of children fully immunized by the age of 2, women's health services and support groups, safety awareness, exercise programs, occupational safety, and many others. Students learned research methods, interviewing and communication techniques, data analysis, how to use data to measure results in the community, technical writing, community involvement, the significance of local culture to health status, and the impact of "outsider versus insider" in community trust. A range of clinical learning activities resulted from programs developed in response to survey results; examples included physical assessment and diagnosis, application of psychomotor skills, implications of nutritional levels on health status, and individual and group teaching.

Community Benefits

Community members were involved in the initial development and revision of the data-collection instrument, served as local guides and mentors to the interview team, and participated in team training. They hosted students as they remained in the community for data collection, and later for learning experiences. Community members became an integral part of the educational process. They assisted in the dissemination of the results of the survey to the community at large through local newspaper, radio, and oral presentations to community organizations. The community learned a great deal about the status of its residents' health and its health-care system. Positive changes, including improvements in socioeconomic status and accessibility of health care, were documented for use by community development groups over the time of the survey.

Research Outcomes

Various research and scholarly outcomes have resulted from this ongoing study and the programs for which its data have provided the foundation. These include national and international presentations by faculty members, a research award by the American Public Health Association section to a faculty member in 1995, a research manuscript accepted for publication in Journal of Rural Health (Beck, Jijon, and Edwards 1995), and others submitted (Burkett and Beck 1990, 1993).

School Nutrition Project

Project Description

A study funded by the College of Nursing of East Tennessee State University links interdisciplinary teaching, service in rural elementary schools, and research. These funds were supplemented by a grant awarded to the Johnson County School System for health education in the area of nutrition. Nursing, public health, and medical students planned, implemented, and evaluated height, weight, blood pressure, and nutrition screening for all elementary school students in Johnson and Hawkins counties. This project is longitudinal, involving students in various years of study in the program and rescreenings to determine changes at specified times.

Student Learning Activities

Students and faculty worked with school officials to plan the intervention program. Interdisciplinary students conducted the screenings; prepared, taught, and evaluated nutrition classes; and arranged for parent follow-up in needed cases. Health professions student learning involved mastery of specific nutritional content, application of knowledge of child development, development of teaching skills, leadership, community collaboration, experience in linking with the referral system in the county in needed cases, and practice of basic health-assessment skills.

Community Benefits

The Johnson County School System was able to compete successfully for a grant award because of the availability of student and faculty involvement to carry out the project. School children received screenings and education never before offered in the county. Parents were actively and enthusiastically involved in improving their children's health. Elementary school children felt better prepared to manage their own health, and many shared their new knowledge with their families.

Research Outcomes

The faculty members were able to obtain funding for a research project that has the potential to lead to external funding in the future. A large data set about the health of rural elementary school children has been collected and, at the completion of the project, will almost certainly result in publication of the results of the intervention study in a peer-reviewed journal (Virgin and Wachs 1995).

Identification and Reduction of Health Risks
Among Employees in a Rural County

Project Description

Johnson County is a poor, rural, and medically underserved county located in the Appalachian Mountains of northeast Tennessee. Long-standing economic challenges and numerous plant closures have been powerful stressors for the workforce. County-wide mortality data reveal greater rates for cardiovascular disease, cancer, and motor vehicle accidents than in the rest of the state or the nation as a whole. Against this challenging backdrop, a two-year employee health risk-assessment and intervention project was designed. A team of nursing, medical, and public and allied health students and faculty collected data on health history, life-style habits, height/weight, blood pressure, and serum cholesterol on nearly a quarter of the county's employed population. Participating companies received a group health-risk profile along with detailed individual reports and risk-reduction information for each employee.

Student Learning Activities

Students used community development and health-assessment skills to organize the project and gather the anthropomorphic and personal health-risk data at the sites. They conducted the quantitative analysis and prepared individual and group reports, working directly with plant management or employee health services in prioritizing the results for intervention efforts. Student teams have begun conducting health education programs at the sites where data analysis is complete. By participating in the project, students have gained practical experience in the research process, interdisciplinary team collaboration, health assessment, planning, communication skills, and community empowerment.

Community Benefits

By the completion of the project, the majority of employees in Johnson County will be given the opportunity to learn about their own health risks and how to lower them. Small and large employers alike will be supported with data to guide health-care cost-containment and prevention strategies. A longitudinal database will be established to measure long-term health needs and changing employee risk status in the future.

Research Outcomes

Preliminary data reveal that Johnson County employees have an overall higher health risk than the national average for employed persons. This is primarily due to the following risk factors: not wearing seat belts, being overweight, high blood pressure, high cholesterol, sedentary living, and smoking cigarettes. Follow-up risk appraisals will determine the impact of risk-reduction interventions in each of these areas (Wachs, Florence, and Virgin 1995).

A Community Partnership in Service to the Homeless: University of Pittsburgh and the City of Pittsburgh

by Thomas P. O'Toole, Joyce Holl, and Paul Freyder

Pittsburgh is a city long known for its industrial prowess, home to industrial giants Carnegie, Mellon, and Westinghouse. It is also a victim of one of the most precipitous industrial declines in American history. Along the banks of the three rivers that geographically define the city — the Allegheny and the Monongahela converging to form the Ohio — lie the skeletons of scores of steel mills and industrial plants. Made obsolete by less expensive overseas steel, antiquated equipment, and declining demand, these rusting relics serve as a grim reminder of how fragile our communities are. More than 100,000 jobs were lost during the 1980s as once-bustling steel-town communities were reduced to modern-day ghost towns inhabited by those too old, infirm, or demonized to adapt to the changing global economy.

But as is true for many great American cities faced with adversity, Pittsburgh too has played the phoenix. Unlike recoveries from fire, flood, or earthquake, this renaissance required much more than rebuilding the physical infrastructure. It also required retooling the human capital of the region. Much of this transformation was ushered in by the biomedical and the health-care service industries. The University of Pittsburgh and its medical center are now the third largest employer in the state. In the city of Braddock, just south of Pittsburgh, U.S. Steel's Edgar Thompson Steel Works employs just over 800 people, followed by Braddock General Hospital, which employs 750.

However, to those men and women unable to adapt, retrain, and take part in the region's transformation, this renaissance came at a significant price. While economic opportunities became available to those able, willing, and afforded the chance, those less capable and disenfranchised found themselves increasingly relying on a social service safety net already stretched thin by the region's precarious history. In addition, the impact of urban violence and trauma, substance abuse, lack of access to affordable and appropriate medical care, and economic distress all have strained the foundation and fabric of our communities. In Pittsburgh, as in other cities, the result has been an increase in homelessness, domestic violence, teen crime and incarceration, and poor health indices and outcomes. Neighborhoods in Pittsburgh rank as some of the poorest in the country, with unemployment rates more than 10 times higher than the region's average. The infant mortality rate in the towns of Homestead and Duquesne, and in the Hill District section of the city is more than 20 per 1,000 live births, compared with fewer than eight in other, more affluent areas. An African-American male living in Pittsburgh has a life expectancy 7.6 years less than his white counterpart.

It is within these challenges of urban decline and turmoil that many of our community partners live, work, and strive to make a difference. The safety net of service providers in Pittsburgh is unique in its strong reliance on volunteer and nonprofit agencies and charitable support. There is a long tradition of a "shared-burden" mentality, typified by the absence of a county public hospital, with all indigent care instead shared among the region's providers. Pittsburgh's industrial legacy has also brought with it some of the nation's most distinguished and well-endowed charitable foundations. This has buttressed the nonprofit and charitable activities of local and regional agencies, fostering innovations in the provision of services and multiple access points to social services. The provider network for homeless care is an example of this relationship. Eight separate agencies — funded by private foundations, federal grants, corporate/public institution programs, or volunteer in-kind donations — are involved in providing health care to the homeless. Services are coordinated by case managers and providers, with a resulting system that maximizes layers of service, avenues for entry, and interagency collaboration. This provider environment has also fostered greater vertical integration of services with the merging of social, health, employment, and family agendas by partners typically separated by bureaucratic and other barriers.

University-assisted service projects have flourished in this environment, in part due to a willingness of community partners to embrace an academic mission within the context of their service-delivery model. It has also flourished because of a recognized need within the health professions schools to broaden the scope of what defines health and where it can be promoted. This is a reflection of the changing economic environment of health care as capitation shifts the focus from facility-driven to population-driven care. It is also a reflection of the changing roles and challenges faced by health providers and the need to respond to societal needs and demands.

The Health Professions Schools in Service to the Nation (HPSISN) project in Pittsburgh is a partnership between the University of Pittsburgh's Program for Health Care to Underserved Populations and the Salvation Army Public Inebriate Program, the Pittsburgh Recovery Center, and the Pittsburgh Women's Center and Shelter. Each of these agencies has a long and distinguished tradition of providing an array of social services to its specific clientele. The HPSISN project builds upon a service-based model by bringing university resources and personnel to the partner agency to provide a community-identified service (i.e., primary health care). The service is provided free of charge and under the direct supervision of a community mentor/agency partner. This is in contrast to learning-based models, where the primary role or function of the university is to place students at sites where they are incorporated into community service teams, with less direct university involvement in the delivery or outcome of projects.

The first partnership developed was with the Salvation Army Public Inebriate Program (PIP) in Southside Pittsburgh. The Salvation Army PIP operates a drop-in center for area homeless, a nonmedical detox unit, a thrift store, and an adult rehabilitation center/long-term shelter for men and women in recovery. In February 1993, we opened a free clinic in the drop-in center that was staffed by internal medicine residents from the University of Pittsburgh Medical Center, first- and second-year medical students, student and community nurses, and pharmacy faculty and students. The program has expanded to now include biweekly health education talks at the shelter, a clinic at the detox unit, and three-day-a-week clinic offerings at the drop-in center. Subsequent partnerships and primary-care clinics have been developed with the Pittsburgh Recovery Center, which provides community outreach and assistance to low-income community residents in recovery, the Pittsburgh Women's Center and Shelter, which provides services to victims of domestic violence, and the Salvation Army–Northside for homeless health care in that community. All care is provided free, including medications; no billing occurs. Almost 4,000 patient-visits are provided annually, with only 1.9 percent of encounters resulting in referral to an emergency department. More than 250 students participated in the program in 1996, and we currently have 70 residents and almost 20 university faculty volunteering at the clinics.

Much of the success achieved within the program stems from some fundamental features that have proved essential. First, all of the clinics are identified by our community partners as their own and provide services identified by them. Sharing ownership within a service-based model is essential to community buy-in. Equally important is that each clinic is run by a community mentor. Not only does this provide legitimacy to the endeavor, but it also operationalizes the shared ownership. Second, our model is based on a premise of voluntarism and giving back to the community. All of our faculty and residents are volunteers. No billing takes place, and an emphasis is placed on meeting a community need and avoiding the politics and hassle that often accompany more traditionally structured care models. This imparts an altruism to our model that students benefit from, that attracts extremely talented, motivated providers and role models, and that provides a useful escape from the increasingly mercantile nature of health care that has disillusioned so many providers.

Finally, we have thus far succeeded in not outgrowing our capacity for sustainment. The demise of many free clinics is often heralded by initial funding successes that cannot be sustained. Keeping overhead, personnel, and expenditures for supplies at a minimum is essential to keeping free care free. The excess capacity that exists in both academic settings and community settings can be redirected without impeding their respective core missions. In our case, we either set up temporary clinics in meeting rooms or use space not in use by the agency. The space is donated and upkeep expenses are absorbed by the host agency, since these costs would have been incurred in any event. Surplus clinical equipment and supplies are donated by the hospital, and medications are donated by either pharmaceutical companies or a local drug store chain.

Sustainment is always an issue and one that means different things to different stakeholders. Within a service-based model, our community partners see sustainment as intrinsically linked to our continued capacity to provide a needed service. While there is a commitment to the education mission and objectives of the university, it is a limited commitment unless the reciprocal service needs are being addressed. This is particularly true when, as in most programs like ours, community mentors and preceptors are not being reimbursed, or not being reimbursed significantly, for the time they spend with students.

Parallel to the service need is a need for feedback and data. Our community partners are often in more precarious financial circumstances and much more tethered to charitable donations and foundation grants than we are. The ability to generate and share data on services provided and their associated outcomes is a value-added service that a university partnership can provide to its community hosts. Likewise, feedback on educational objectives and student evaluations is important, and helps validate the energies devoted to teaching by both the community mentors and the volunteer faculty.

Our academic stakeholders, course chairpersons, academic deans, and the curriculum committee also have a vested interest in meaningful outcomes. Sustainment from a university perspective is contingent on demonstrating that the service exercise meets the educational objectives of a rigorous curriculum and that students appreciate the experience in the process. We have found it essential to, first and foremost, not overstate what service activities can accomplish. The misgivings of basic science faculty about the prospect of losing classroom time to what they perceive as a "fluff" experience are difficult to overcome, and the educational and experiential objectives of a service experience need to be clearly articulated.

We have developed two methods of evaluation to help ensure program sustainability. First, students complete an experience-specific assessment that focuses on project goals and objectives and student satisfaction with their experience. Second, we conduct a survey on global attitudes and perceptions of care to the underserved with the premise of demonstrating the impact of service on perceptions of community needs and social responsibilities. Direct feedback of these data to clinic preceptors, course chairpersons, and academic deans is critical to sustaining institutional support.

Finally, the importance of catering to the needs and objectives of the students participating cannot be overstated. The ultimate success of the project is contingent upon engaged, interested students. Tailoring service experiences to match student levels of comfort, expertise, and education is essential. Equally important is the need to offer alternative service opportunities with different special-need populations to accommodate specific student interests. Both hands-on activities and student leadership are integral components of a successful program, and both enhance the service and facilitate the process. We have been very fortunate in being able to work closely with a student organization, the Homeless Outreach and Education Program (HOEP), that has been essential to the planning of new service projects, garnering student interest, and providing useful and timely feedback.

Our HPSISN program has been the result of a combination of good luck, good timing, understanding and patient community partners, and committed faculty and students. Although the first four years have seen tremendous growth in interest and involvement at both the university and community levels, the next four are likely to hold different and more pressing challenges. Specific hurdles we will need to overcome are related to our continuing efforts to maintain a free-care, volunteer-based clinic structure. Equally important will be finding creative ways to access services, as tapping into surplus resources becomes more difficult. Adapting the curriculum to problem-based and other module-styled learning approaches will provide both challenges and opportunities. Even more challenging will be our ability to sustain the program within a context of increasing managed care and contracted physician services. Emphasizing personal, professional, and institutional missions as well as a sense of social responsibility will be essential.

In summary, we have developed a model that is service-based, community-responsive, and driven by those who elect to contribute to it. It has worked well in Pittsburgh but is also replicable at other institutions and communities. Most important, it has provided a link within our communities to the university and has brought health professionals at all levels back to the communities that define our very diverse city.

Student-Initiated Community Service:
The Community Health Advancement Program

by Sharon Dobie, Bonnie Beck, Melinda Tonelli, Charlene Forslund, Connie Huffine, Deborah Kippen, Diane Demopulos, and William Hobson

The Community Health Advancement Program (CHAP) began at the University of Washington in 1980 to encourage medical students to consider careers working with underserved populations. CHAP sponsors student-run extracurricular community service projects and a seminar series. Each program is a collaborative effort among the students, the Department of Family Medicine, and a Seattle-area community-based agency. CHAP seeks to develop programs that address an identifiable unmet need in a local underserved community.

The first CHAP program was the Saturday Clinic at Holly Park Community Health Center, located in a low-income housing project in Seattle. The health center was open only on weekdays, but the multiethnic patients of the health center often needed to obtain care on weekends. The health center was unable to fill the need for the expanded hours. At the same time, a group of students at the medical school, disillusioned with the amount of time spent learning basic sciences, wanted to provide a community service and to develop clinical skills. CHAP was born from the match between the needs of the health center and the aspirations of the students. It provided the community with a needed service and the students with an avenue for expressing and living their values. It provided the volunteer faculty with a locus for teaching community-oriented primary care, leadership skills, and cross-cultural medicine.

After starting the Saturday Clinic, CHAP piloted several other programs with variable success. By the late 1980s, the two CHAP programs that remained and flourished were the CHAP Saturday Clinic and a Brown-Bag Luncheon Speaker series on community health topics. Each had a program structure, support, and the ability to continue and replace leaders annually. Both had modest or no need for funding. During the late 1980s, student interest in CHAP increased. In the 1990s, CHAP expanded to include not only the Saturday Clinic but also a flu shot clinic for the elderly, a pre-sports physical clinic for low-income middle and high school athletes, a cooking project for home-bound persons with AIDS, a dermatology clinic for the homeless in a downtown shelter, a diabetic education and foot-care project, and two pilot programs tutoring and mentoring adolescents (see table). Two programs, the CHAP Saturday Clinic and the Chicken Soup Brigade cooking project for HIV-infected homebound individuals, have ended. In both cases,

CHAP Projects

Program	Description	Years of Operation	Community Partner	# Coordinators Per Year	# Volunteers Per Year
Saturday Clinic	A weekly primary-care clinic	1982-1996	Rainier Park Community Health Center	10	288
Brown-Bag Series	Seminar with community leaders	1983 - current	Various community-based presenters	2-4	230
Flu Shot Clinic	Immunizations for elderly	1987 - current	Rainier Park Community Health Center	4	28
Sports Medicine Clinic	Pre-sports physicals for teens	1987 - current	Foster High School, Renton High School	4	20-30
Chicken Soup Brigade Project	Cooking for persons living with AIDS	1993-1995	Chicken Soup Brigade	4	120
Dermatology Clinic	Dermatology care for sheltered homeless adults	1995 - current	Downtown Emergency Service Center and Pioneer Square Clinic	8	72
Teen Activities	Tutoring homeless teens	1997 - current	Orion Center	4	8-28
Adolescent Mentoring	Middle school student mentoring	1997 - current	Seattle Public Schools	6	15-60
Diabetic Education and Foot Care	Foot care and patient education for diabetics	1997 - current	Rainier Park Community Health Center	2	10

the cosponsoring community agencies became able to provide services that rendered the CHAP program no longer necessary.

CHAP programs are student-initiated, student-designed, and student-administered. Strategies to obtain financial support are also developed by the students, most of whom have been medical students. Technical assistance, leadership training, and sponsorship are provided by faculty and staff in the Department of Family Medicine, University of Washington School of Medicine, and by the cosponsoring community agency. The students spend anywhere from six months to two years in the needs-assessment and development phase of new projects; during this time, they meet regularly with the community cosponsors and with CHAP faculty. In addition to supervising student volunteers during program sessions, student coordinators meet regularly to administer their programs. All student coordinators for CHAP programs meet together quarterly to discuss programs and to address concerns. Each year, student leaders recruit their replacements and assist in training them.

All CHAP programs share six basic tenets that must be satisfied prior to the opening of a new program. First, no student-run program will succeed without highly interested students. Second, programs must develop from unmet needs defined by the community and the agencies serving it. Third, prior to implementation, a program must develop the tools and processes to be used in implementing, supporting, evaluating, and modifying it. Fourth, programs must link to ongoing services within the community. Fifth, programs must provide a vehicle for students to learn as they serve. Sixth, all programs must be evaluated regularly.

The story of CHAP's growth and development is the focus of the remainder of this paper. To illustrate the first five of the above six principles, it will describe how a new CHAP program develops, using the CHAP dermatology clinic as an example. It will then describe the sixth principle — the necessity of evaluation — by highlighting the evaluation of the CHAP Saturday Clinic that led to its closure. For CHAP to thrive, three groups of people, very often with different but overlapping goals and interests, must enthusiastically work together. Students serve as leaders, managing the CHAP programs, and as volunteers. The community agencies provide the direct link to the underserved communities, identifying unmet needs and often providing institutional and programmatic support. The Department of Family Medicine provides staff and faculty support, mentoring, and leadership training.

Methods for Building and Sustaining Programs:
The CHAP Dermatology Clinic

During orientation to medical school and at a Department of Family Medicine fair in early October, entering students learn about CHAP and sign up as volunteers. Students who are interested in working with underserved populations often visit the departmental office to discuss ideas, programs, and opportunities for involvement. New programs start with a group of students who share an interest in working with a particular community or program. Periodically, students are invited to participate in a retreat to discuss CHAP and its programs.

In October 1992, all CHAP student coordinators and other interested medical, undergraduate, and graduate students attended a retreat with CHAP faculty and staff. During this retreat, the students were enthusiastic about developing a program to serve the homeless. With a community and a group of highly motivated students already identified, a needs assessment could begin.

Between October 1992 and July 1993, a series of meetings was held with staff from the Downtown Emergency Service Center (DESC) and from the Pioneer Square Clinic, a satellite of the Harborview Medical Center. Both are located in the same neighborhood; DESC is a shelter and the Pioneer Square Clinic is the primary provider of medical services to the homeless population in the downtown and Pioneer Square areas of Seattle. These service agencies defined dermatological illnesses as a significant unmet health need for the homeless. Without such a community base, students might well have identified a different focus for their activities with the homeless, in all likelihood, one that would not have addressed a defined unmet need. Furthermore, in the process of meeting with agency staff, the students learned valuable lessons in collaboration and clarification of expectations.

Between July 1993 and November 1994, a working group of three — and at times more — students, with advice from the medical director of the Pioneer Square Clinic, the administrative staff from DESC, and CHAP faculty and staff, developed the program. Prior to implementation, the working group had to project a continuing need in the community, available funding, staffing (students and supervising physicians), procedures and plans for the project, and a mechanism to transition student leadership annually. Program structure, funding, and administrative protocols were also defined by the students. The collaborating community agencies ultimately determined that the proposed program was appropriate and feasible. They reviewed all materials to be certain that the new service was consistent with the goals and standards of DESC and the Pioneer Square Clinic, and could be implemented with the resources brought by CHAP. DESC donated the site: three small rooms in the shelter to serve as examination rooms and a central office. Two Wednesday evenings a month were selected for the actual work. At these times, students would be out of class, clients would be present, and a registered nurse would be on duty.

Funding was needed for supplies and medications. Student leaders developed funding support by meeting with interested individuals and groups. Funding is currently provided by the Harborview Medical Center, the Turner Foundation at the University of Washington, and the Junior League of Seattle. Additionally, CHAP has held garage sales, a toothbrush drive, and a clothing and underwear drive to obtain needed items and to gain support for its efforts.

Detailed clinic protocols were written and revised monthly during the first year of operation. These, for example, included, among other items, job descriptions, how to gain access to the center, how to clean the counters, protocols for creating and reviewing charts, and the management of medical emergencies. Each clinic session was staffed by student coordinators, two teams of two students each (a preclinical and a clinical student), and an attending physician. Coordinators held their positions for a year. Other students were asked to volunteer for a quarter to increase provider continuity. A lottery was used to select students from the large number who were interested. A student coordinator recruited supervising physicians from the faculty and the community.

Through their work with community agencies, CHAP student leaders learn that the services they provide are only a small piece of a much larger fabric of service. For the dermatology clinic, links were developed with the Harborview Dermatology Service, the Pioneer Square Clinic, and Harborview Hospital. A referral process was established for general medical conditions, as well as for dermatological problems beyond the scope or expertise of the clinic. Clients could be referred to the Pioneer Square Clinic the next day or, if necessary, to the Harborview Emergency Room that night. The clinic also had direct access to dermatology appointments at Harborview within five days of an evening clinic.

Student learning in the CHAP program is multidimensional. Student coordinators learn administrative and planning skills through each phase of program development, implementation, management, and evaluation. All volunteering students learn clinical skills through program orientations and while providing direct service. CHAP faculty and staff provide leadership and administrative education, mentor coordinators, and train and orient volunteers.

In the case of the dermatology clinic, student coordinators and volunteers were given a half-day orientation to the DESC and to working with homeless adults. Students also attended a seminar once a quarter on health and the homeless. While their service involvement was voluntary, students could nonetheless receive one elective credit for participating in the seminar. At the clinic, students received from the supervising physician and nurse instruction that was relevant both to the particular patients they saw and to broader issues of homelessness.

Evaluation of CHAP Programs: The CHAP Saturday Clinic Story

The CHAP evaluation system can be adapted to each CHAP program. It is student-centered and community-based. It was designed with three main objectives. First, the evaluation sought to clarify student and community agency goals, identify areas of unmet community need, and design program modifications to better achieve the stated goals. This would ensure that the program being evaluated met the needs of both the community and the students. Second, we hoped to develop a collaborative evaluation process that would enhance the service linkage between the medical school and the community. Third, the evaluation process sought to provide students with practical experience in needs assessment. Led by a student evaluator, evaluations would be conducted primarily through focus-group discussions with all constituencies. Evaluation of the CHAP Saturday Clinic at the Community Health Center illustrates the value of this method.

When the CHAP Saturday Clinic was first established in 1983, the Community Health Center had limited hours of operation. The CHAP Saturday Clinic filled an unmet need by allowing the center to expand the hours of available medical care in the community. Since 1982, the health center has grown dramatically and has expanded its hours. It now operates its own Saturday clinic, which, for a time, was run concurrently with the CHAP clinic. Ongoing evaluation of the CHAP Saturday Clinic allowed health center staff and CHAP students and staff to critically assess whether the CHAP Saturday Clinic continued to meet the goals of participating groups.

The lead student evaluator facilitated structured focus-group discussions with both the student coordinators and the health center staff in order to define the goals of each group, rank the success of the Saturday Clinic in meeting those goals, and generate a list of possible program modifications. These one- to two-hour structured discussions focused on individual, team, and agency goals rather than on the day-to-day running of the clinic.

The Community Health Center had three goals in working with CHAP. First, it wanted CHAP to enhance and expand the services of the center. Second, it wanted to encourage students to choose primary-care careers with underserved populations. Last, it wanted to increase collaboration with

CHAP and integration of CHAP into health center operations.

The student coordinators for the CHAP Saturday Clinic listed four primary goals. First, they wanted to provide a community service. Second, they wanted exposure to medically underserved populations. Third, they wanted to develop leadership, organizational, and communication skills. Last, they wanted to practice clinical skills in a real-world setting.

Each group then evaluated whether and to what extent the Saturday Clinic met these goals. Providing a community service and meeting an unmet need were the most important goals for the students. CHAP staff, health center staff, and the CHAP students all agreed that the Saturday Clinic no longer met this goal. All perceived the Saturday Clinic as primarily an educational experience for the students. Enhancing health center services, which was the most important goal for the health center staff, was also not being achieved. Since the health center was now open on Saturdays, the CHAP Saturday Clinic did not enhance services by operating at the same time. Three secondary goals, however, were being met successfully by the CHAP Saturday Clinic. Students were (1) working with the medically underserved and (2) developing clinical skills, while (3) student coordinators were learning leadership skills.

Through this evaluation process, the student coordinators and health center staff recommended that the CHAP Saturday Clinic be adapted to more effectively meet the goals of each group. They recommended that any CHAP program at the health center be one that enhances the health center's mission. It was important for the CHAP program not to be viewed as a burden to health center staff. The health center suggested that CHAP consider developing a clinic with a focus on a targeted patient population with an unmet need. Diabetic foot care, asthma education, and support for young, new mothers were mentioned as possibilities.

The student coordinators recommended that they conduct a limited needs assessment within the health center and its service community, and with several other targeted agencies throughout the city. The information garnered from the assessment, coupled with areas of student interest, would provide the basis for modification of the CHAP Saturday Clinic. This might mean a change in the clinic's focus, the clinic's move to a new site with unmet needs, or the development of an entirely new program at a new site.

Discussion

CHAP has evolved during its years of service. It has grown in the number and breadth of programs it manages. During the last five years, CHAP has clarified methods for program development and used these methods to develop at least four new programs. CHAP has also implemented an evaluation program that can track whether a program continues to meet the goals of the constituencies involved. It also provides information useful for program modification. Last, CHAP has become more conscious in its efforts to mentor student leaders and provide leadership training.

All CHAP programs demonstrate the principles and structure important to developing student-run, extracurricular service programs. Students must be enthusiastic and interested, or they will not devote the time necessary to develop a program. Programs are best linked to agencies with programs in the communities of interest. These communities and the agencies serving them can best define areas of unmet need; dialogue between students and agencies can clarify which areas are amenable to a student-run program. In the example of the dermatology clinic, students wished to serve the homeless. The DESC and the Pioneer Square Clinic identified skin problems as a large unmet need.

Significant time is needed for planning and development prior to implementation. Students are eager to be in the community and serving. But the time spent in building community connections and defining an infrastructure that can be funded and supported for several years is critical. For example, planning for the dermatology clinic took two years. Such planning efforts provide extremely important learning opportunities for student coordinators.

Last, students often volunteer because they wish to *serve*. It is equally important to identify *learning* goals for students. For student volunteer providers, these might include not only clinical experiences but also topics such as the health concerns of the particular target community, social services available to the community, and other topics. Student coordinators have an interest in such topics but also in planning, administration, health services, and health policy.

Evaluation is an important component of a successful program. Clearly, community need is not a stagnant variable, nor are relationships with the community and agencies serving it. Ongoing dialogue and formal annual evaluations allow programs to change and grow as needed by the community. Furthermore, the involvement of students in the evaluation process provides additional opportunity for reflection upon initial goals and learning experiences gained through participation. Last, as demonstrated by the evaluation of the CHAP Saturday Clinic, the process can lead to significant changes in a CHAP program.

The CHAP Saturday Clinic has had a long and successful history. All of the collaborators were highly invested in the program. Making substantive changes in this type of well-established, well-supported program is difficult. Change requires the support of all the collaborators. This evaluation model, which focused on individual team and agency goals rather than on the mechanics of running the clinic, provided an opportunity for the student evaluators to determine whether the program was meeting the needs for which it was designed. Through the evaluation process, it became evident that although the Saturday Clinic was still providing an excellent educational opportunity for students, it was no longer meeting an unmet need in the community, nor was it meeting the students' goal of providing a needed community service. Such a process reinforces a basic premise of CHAP: Service programs based in the community cannot be static. Programs need the flexibility to adapt, modify, or relocate as needs change.

CHAP remains committed to service and to learning through providing service. It represents a dynamic opportunity for students. Those who volunteer learn much about the community they are serving. Those who lead learn even more. Student-managed programs can thrive, be a vehicle for students to learn as they serve, and provide meaningful contributions to the community.

The Socialization of Medical Students in a Preventive Health Service-Learning Experience

by JoEllen Tarallo-Falk

This research examines how service-learning promotes preventive health practice in medical education. The research is based on a study of medical students who participated in a service-learning program at Dartmouth Medical School called "Partners in Health Education" (see Walsh et al. elsewhere in this volume). The program places medical students in public schools to work with teachers on the delivery of health education and prevention programs. The study examines the medical student perspective on the experience, applies a sociological framework to medical education, and considers the impact of this experience on medical student socialization into the medical profession. The study on which the research conclusions are based employs the analysis of 36 primary and follow-up interviews conducted over a two-year period, medical student journals and papers, program evaluation data, and observation (Tarallo-Falk 1995).

Socialization research in medicine examines the factors that function specifically to influence medical students' future behavior in the physician role. This involves understanding how medical students interpret their training experiences, and requires exploring the meanings they assign to the events in which they are enmeshed. The learning of attitudes, norms, values, beliefs, and behavior patterns is of prime interest, as are the knowledge and skills taught overtly in the curriculum. In general, the literature indicates that there is still much to be concerned about regarding the professional socialization of physicians (Tarallo-Falk 1994).

During medical training, students learn a set of professional attitudes, values, and behaviors through which they come to relate themselves as doctors to others in society. These perspectives guide their actions as physicians. They reflect the values, attitudes, and behavioral experiences that medical students bring to situations, as well as the values and attitudes operating in the social environments influential in their development.

This article examines how the medical students thought their experiences in the Partners program had influenced them, especially with regard to their roles as doctors. Regardless of the many practical and logistical program issues that created conflict for the students, they remained enthusiastic about the practical experience the program offers. The heart of Partners, according to many students, is "the experiential learning," and the value of Partners is that it provides "the humanitarian aspects of medical school."

These humanitarian aspects contribute to increasing the self-esteem and confidence of the medical students at a vulnerable time in their professional development. They affirm for the students that they are contributing members of society, thus helping them to "stay in touch with humanity" and focusing their energies on thinking about and building skills for relationships with people.

The Anticipatory Socialization of Future Physician-Teachers

Every student made some reference to the impact that participation in Partners might have on her or his future perspectives and role as a physician. This phenomenon of anticipatory socialization (Merton 1982) can be described in two major ways. First, the Partners experience places students in situations that demand performance in a new professional situation. As such, it contributes to role-setting, a process whereby the student begins to think and act in ways appropriate to the role she or he is assuming in the situation. Second, it provides the context by which the student actually practices new technical and social skills, thereby facilitating skill building and preparing her or him for performance.

Students made numerous references to the perceived impact of the experience on role-setting: "It gave me comfort with being an educator, which I feel is an important part of being a good physician." "I think that, number one, it reminds me of what I think part of my role is . . . to help people understand their health better, not just necessarily to treat their disease." In addition, students related what they were learning to future performance: "It makes me think of questions I should be asking during a medical interview." "The 'teachable moment,' what an invaluable tool that will be when I am in the intimacy of the doctor-patient relationship!" The following student discussed the impact of considering the social context of a patient's life when treating a patient:

> I think it would be worth knowing any kind of social things that would have been a factor in what is going on with them [future patients]. I would like them to be able to go beyond the physical and discuss what is going on in their lives.

Finally, some students perceived that the experience would have a ripple effect, expanding beyond the current setting and players. The following student projected how the experience might inform her role in her own family, as a doctor, and in the community:

> I also maintained the classroom atmosphere, the discipline aspect, and I

think that is going to be helpful even for my own family, when I grow up (laughter) and have a family. And it would be very helpful for me to advise other parents. Sometimes I know that parents do consider doctors as people they can get advice from . . . like "My kid is hyperactive, how do I deal with that?" or "My kid just won't relate with other kids, how do I deal with that?" And working with these kids, and working with the teacher who is an expert on child psychology and the ins and outs of how to work with children, really gave me much more of a perspective of how to work with kids, how to discipline kids. So I can pass that on to parents in the future if they come into my office.

Importance in the Early Stages of Professional Development

Students discussed the particular importance of doing service early in their development as doctors. They believed that exposure to the community and service work is timely for medical students, who are mostly in their 20s, because "it is a time when the self is still forming who it is." These experiences "could tip them toward having positive attitudes about service" and could "set a precedent early in [their] career to participate in the community." The idea of "being in the service of the community" was mentioned frequently (n=12) as part of a doctor's role. The students described this as an important part of their anticipatory socialization, because "what you are doing by getting involved with the community at this stage is going to be helpful to you, and prepare you for your work in some ways." Here is how one student discussed the formative impact of participation in the program:

> *It seems to be a wonderful time to do something like this. As I said before, you're still more in the patient's perspective than anything else. So I think it is very good, very formative. It's like how they say . . . most people spend the next 50 years of their life fixing the first five. I think probably the same is true for medicine and the foundation you receive there. I think this was a very positive, formative experience for the beginning of a medical education. . . . I tell people about it and how great it is, how I learned to communicate a little bit better, and how I enjoyed being with children and the role I play in the community. I think those are all giving you a taste of upcoming responsibilities as a doctor in almost any area that you go into.*

How the Partners Experience Affects the Current Academic Program

Some students made explicit connections between their experience in the Partners program and their academic work during the first two years of medical school. Other students initially responded that there were no direct academic connections. However, upon conversing, every student ultimately made some direct or indirect academic connection. The following statement exemplifies this complicated train of thought:

> Academically, I don't think it helps at all. I really don't. For some people and in certain subject areas, it might help you clarify concepts if you go back and you are teaching something. . . . I taught them about spinal cord injuries, and I went back and looked at my neuroanatomy notes and sort of became reacquainted with them and figured out how to teach them to third graders. I probably gained a little clearer understanding for myself, but I don't think that is a big part of it. I think that in terms of skills and communication skills, it is very helpful. I think in terms of social responsibility, it is very helpful, and it is a good outlet.

Students also made their own value judgments about time spent in the Partners program versus other academic requirements. On the posttraining survey, one student wrote: "On the whole, the teaching aspect of the program, the time I was in the classroom, was a better investment of my time than studying . . . honestly!"

The Partners program provides students with a context for experiential learning. That context facilitates both the application and the extension of relevant knowledge, attitudes, and skills.

Applied Learning

Students identified two major ways that their academic learning was applied through participation in Partners. First, the context of the program provided "a grounding for the medical students as they go about learning information." It furnished the opportunity to take what they have learned in the basic sciences and relearn it in such a way that they can teach it to someone else. This facilitated their learning the material even more effectively: "I found that my understanding of immunology was immeasurably better because I had to explain it to high school kids who wouldn't have understood, you know, a lot of those tests or those little individual points."

Further, teaching the material required they translate the information into concepts and a language understandable to the lay audience. Communication skills were identified as a major outcome of participation in the program and are discussed below. "It allowed me to see what I was doing in school could be translated into important information. It forced me to put into words what we learn in school."

Second, learning was also applied through the development of "practical knowledge and experience." These experiences allowed students to "get close up and comfortable" with issues related to their academic learning. A student explained:

> It sort of drives the point home that these are very important issues. It is easy to sit in class; we're taking growth and development right now, and we're dealing with a lot of these issues, adolescence and middle childhood and development and such. It is all well and good to sit in class and learn about it and read someone else's work, but when you go out there and you interact with these kids . . . it brings the point home that in fact this really is [what] some of the important issues out in the community [are].

Extended Learning

Academic learning was also extended through participation in the program. Students identified three ways this learning occurred: (1) acquiring new, but medically relevant material; (2) practicing new skills; and (3) expanding their perspective.

Medically relevant information. Students mentioned (n=14) that the program provided multiple opportunities to learn new, but medically relevant material not taught in the medical education curriculum. One student provided an example: "The experience motivated me to do some learning about current nutrition information not taught in the medical school curriculum."

New skills. Students were introduced to, practiced, and/or learned a variety of new skills. Skill learning was identified (n=26) as a major outcome of participation in the program. The major skills students reported learning include communication, recognition of social factors contributing to disease, and health education skills, such as understanding developmental issues. (These are discussed in the next section.) In some cases, students felt the program had given them significant opportunity to develop these skills. In other cases, students felt the experience had pushed them, to varying degrees, along a continuum of skill development already in progress.

Expanded perspective. Students (n=26) reported that the experience had helped expand their perspective through interpersonal experience in a new social context. As Schön notes (1987: 241), the service-learning experience provides a virtual world, a constructed representation of real worlds of practice, both their own and that of other professionals. A student explained:

> All of the book work you do and all the lecture sitting that you do is going to eventually be replaced by interacting with people, and this for me was a

light at the end of the tunnel: Why we are doing all this stuff? What is behind this disease? Well, there is a person behind it, and I just thought that it was the interpersonal, call it clinical, aspect of all of the scientific learning that we do. [Service] was my substitute for clinical experience in my first year.

For the students, seeing the issues firsthand was more valuable than learning theory. The theory wouldn't make any sense "if you never saw the kinds of things that happen" in the real world. Learning by doing, seeing, and therefore understanding raised their level of awareness to a new level of concern. This in turn informed the development of attitudes and values that may be beneficial to the future doctor and to the community. Another student discussed this:

These opportunities assist in the development of their own future servant attitude because of their understanding of how a community works, because of, I guess, the fact that their perspective is a little broader. When I say that the perspective is a little bit broader, I mean that they have an idea of how they can fit into the community when they finish their schooling.

The Perception and Indicators of Impact

It was important to students (n=19) that their participation in Partners resulted in some level of impact, whether on themselves or others. This was precipitated by the underlying value and belief that their time in service "should make a difference." They looked for evidence — indicators or non-indicators — that they had or had not had an impact. Students identified indicators of impact on themselves as including a feeling of connection or bonding, an increase in their own confidence or self-esteem, and any of the outcomes of applied or extended learning. When students successfully identified indicators of impact, they experienced purpose in the service work. The experience of personal purpose reinforced the value and belief that they could make a difference.

Indicators of the impact of the experience on the students themselves included a feeling of connection and/or bonding, increased confidence and/or self-esteem, and outcomes of applied or extended learning — the acquisition of practical knowledge, new skills, and expanded perspectives. Indicators of the impact on others included connection/bonding, role-modeling, children's demonstrating new knowledge, attitudes, and behaviors, and feedback from teachers, parents, children, and the program administration.

Generally, the medical students were confident their time in the classroom resulted in a fun experience for themselves and their pupils, but they were less certain about whether they had actually had an impact on high school student learning. They began to recognize limits to their potential sphere of influence. Some medical students also realized they were not going to be able to accomplish what they had hoped to. The following student's train of thought illustrates how the process of questioning his impact made him think about his role in a larger system of prevention:

> Sometimes I wondered how much of an impact this information would really have on the way they chose to eat. I guess this is what I mean about keeping the big picture in mind when you are only one person teaching one small unit. You just have to hope that the kids have absorbed what you've told them, and they get help from others too, so they can use the information to make choices for the rest of their lives.

Conclusion

The phenomenon of anticipatory socialization (Merton 1982), whereby students describe how participation in Partners will have an impact on their future perspectives and roles as physicians, has been described. Their work in schools in collaboration with other professionals (teachers, counselors, nurses) and children, learning to teach about health in developmentally relevant and appropriate ways, required that they respond to new and complex professional situations. This provided the context in which the student actually practiced new technical and social skills, thereby building his or her skills, and preparing him or her for performance. Students felt this experience was particularly valuable in the early stages of their development as doctors.

Every student ultimately made some direct or indirect connection between the experience in the Partners in Health Education preventive health service-learning program and his or her academic work and/or medical practice. The Partners program provided students with a context for experiential learning. This context facilitated both the *application* and the *extension* of relevant knowledge, attitudes, and skills. "Applied" and "extended learning" are descriptors of the way medical students described their learning experiences in the program.

References

Merton, R.K. (1982). *Social Research and the Practicing Professions*. Cambridge, MA: Abt Books.

Schön, D.A. (1987). *Educating the Reflective Practitioner.* San Francisco, CA: Jossey-Bass.

Tarallo-Falk, J. (1994). "Socializing Medical Students: Traditional and Innovative Curriculum Approaches." Qualifying paper, Harvard Graduate School of Education.

——— . (1995). "The Socialization of Medical Students in a Preventive Health Service-Learning Experience." Dissertation, Harvard Graduate School of Education.

Evaluating the Impact of Service-Learning:
Applications for Medical Education

by Sherril B. Gelmon, Barbara Holland, Beth Morris, and Amy Driscoll

Health professions educators seek to improve the relevance of their educational programs to meet community needs and ultimately contribute to improving the health of the communities and populations they serve. As health-services delivery increasingly shifts to a managed-care model, career patterns of many health professionals are moving away from traditional affiliations with large institutional complexes to community-based delivery settings. These new career patterns and delivery environments call for a change in educational preparation so that students are prepared to succeed in these new settings.

One of these changes is the integration of service-learning into health professions education in general, and into medical education in particular. As service-learning activities increase, faculty and university administrators will be called upon to demonstrate the impact of this pedagogical approach to education. While work in the community — and service — has always been given great value and support in medical education, the actual integration of community-based service as an important part of the academic curriculum has received little attention. Even less attention has been paid to understanding the impact of this educational methodology — the impact on the medical student, on the faculty member, on educational and training institutions, and on the community partners who host students.

This paper describes a model and specific methods for assessing the impact of service-learning in medical education. It draws upon assessment research in general education at Portland State University, and upon the further experience of a Portland State University team in designing and conducting the overall evaluation of the Health Professions Schools in Service to the Nation (HPSISN) program — a national demonstration project testing the effect of integrating service-learning into health professions curricula in 19 university settings across the United States.

The Need for an Assessment Model

Service-learning is an educational methodology that combines community service with explicit academic learning objectives, preparation, and reflection. Students participating in service-learning are expected to provide direct community service, to learn about and reflect upon the community context in which service is provided, and to understand the connection between the service and their academic coursework. These experiences are developed through collaborations between the community and educational programs, relying upon partnerships that address mutual needs. Structured reflection and careful collaboration are two features that differentiate service-learning from practical clinical learning experiences common to health professions education. Furthermore, integration of service-learning into health professions curricula holds great promise for reforming health professions education in ways that correspond to the new career paths created by an emerging health system shaped in large part by managed care.

A major institutional barrier to integrating and sustaining service-learning in health professions education is a lack of systematic and objective evaluation data documenting the impact of service on students, on faculty, on institutions, and on the community itself (Giles, Honnet, and Migliore 1991). Eyler and Giles (1994) point out that the outcomes of service-learning have not been clearly conceptualized, and that there is a lack of agreement about institutional intent in promoting service-learning as a component of the academic experience. Such dissension and lack of clarity have contributed to the lack of significant progress in the development of assessment measures that has, until recently, marked the field. Now, however, evidence illustrating early experiences with practical assessment measures in general education and in health professions education is beginning to develop (Driscoll et al. 1996; Gelmon, Holland, Kerrigan, and Driscoll 1996; Gelmon, Holland, and Morris 1996; Gelmon, Seifer, Holland, and Connors 1996).

The issue of multiple constituencies is a major challenge to the task of assessing service-learning if institutions are to evaluate effectively the full ramifications of their commitment to this approach (Driscoll et al. 1996). The evaluation model implemented in the HPSISN program seeks to capture and disseminate case studies and recommendations of principles of good practice describing service-learning in health professions education (Gelmon, Holland, and Morris 1996). The development of impact data from the HPSISN sites will help demonstrate the educational value of service-learning and further extend its application. In the following sections, we illustrate how the HPSISN evaluation model can be applied throughout medical education — whether the service-learning experiences are within a single discipline or are interdisciplinary.

Measuring the Impact of Service-Learning

In order to understand the development of this assessment model, it is important to recognize the unique context in which we conducted our initial design work. Portland State University (PSU), an urban institution, had recently reformed its undergraduate curriculum in an effort to fulfill its mission to better accommodate a nontraditional student population and to promote research on effective teaching and learning. Service-learning was integrated throughout the new general-education curriculum in freshman experiences, specific service-learning courses, and graduation requirements. This comprehensive approach to the integration of community service influenced the design of the institution's assessment model.

The newness of the service-learning effort and its comprehensive impact across campus called for an exploratory and formative assessment approach. Aware that our enthusiasm and claims must give way to hard data and demonstrated outcomes, and committed to creating a "culture of evidence" at Portland State (Ramaley 1996), we set out to document our reform efforts systematically. This meant that our model would have to ensure the collection of assessment data that could provide feedback for continuous improvement and demonstrate sufficient breadth to serve the diverse forms of service-learning in our curriculum. The design would also have to honor PSU's commitment to mutually beneficial partnerships with the community and, therefore, provide data of value to its community partners.

PSU's mission — to contribute meaningfully to the community's capacity to address local issues and concerns while enhancing the educational experiences of its students — is not unlike that seen in most universities engaged in health professions education, and is certainly reflective of the missions articulated by medical schools and their host academic health centers. However, it is the mutuality of the intended benefits of partnership that is the essence of the service-learning commitment — doing "with" the community rather than doing "for" or doing "to," both of which are more traditional for health professions educators.

There is currently much discussion as to how to assess the impact of service-learning but little research or literature providing models and approaches (Holland et al. 1996). Since the partnership concept that PSU embraces is the essence of its urban mission, a commitment to assessing the experiences and impact for multiple constituencies was, necessarily, a guiding principle of this study.

From the start, we realized we needed to define outcomes for our community-based learning courses — specific outcomes regarding the effects of service-learning on all participants. Much of our development work became a matter of defining desired impacts: What did such impacts look like? How could we establish their presence? We have presented elsewhere a detailed description of our process for understanding these questions (Driscoll et al. 1996).

In part, the assessment model we adopted can be seen to derive from a theoretical base in continuous improvement, and relies on the Model for Improvement that is used extensively in industry, health care, and education (Langley, Nolan, and Nolan 1994). Implementing service-learning requires the creation of a new curricular environment designed to improve learning for students and increase community capacity; it is, therefore, appropriate to build an assessment model that can capture actual changes (impact), if any, and contribute to continuous improvement of partnership strategies. We can usually answer the question as to *how* service-learning is conducted; we can almost always answer *why* service-learning is part of the curriculum. But we can rarely answer the question *how can we improve* this part of the curriculum. This inability to complete the improvement cycle may be a function of not sufficiently understanding the impact of these learning experiences (Gelmon et al. 1995). The Model for Improvement asks three fundamental questions:

1. What are we trying to accomplish?
2. How will we know that a change is an improvement?
3. What change(s) can we make that will result in further improvement?

The following discussion of applications in medical education rests upon a refinement of the assessment model developed around these questions.

An Approach to Evaluation of Service-Learning in Medical Education

Why would medical educators seek to evaluate their service-learning initiatives? Key motivators are the ability to provide evidence of the serviceability of service-learning, as well as to document its impact on multiple constituents, thereby providing a foundation for future curricular reform.

The evaluation model of the interdisciplinary HPSISN program employs a design that assesses the impact service-learning has on each key constituency: community, students, faculty, and institution. There are five research questions that span the program objectives. For each research question, the general purpose is defined and supported by key variables ("What will we look for?") and the indicators that will be used to measure change in the variables ("What will be measured?"). Mechanisms for collecting data to measure the indicators are suggested ("How will it be measured?"). These research questions, purposes, key variables, measurement indicators, and suggested data-collection mechanisms, as modified for applications in medical education, are illustrated in the following pages.

Research Question 1

**How has service-learning affected university-community partnerships
with respect to medical education?**

Purpose:
        To understand the influence of service-learning on the nature and scope of university-community partnerships.

Phenomena to Be Studied:
        Nature of university-community partnerships:
- role of community partners in service-learning
- involvement of community partners in service-learning
- university-community interactions
- nature of services provided

What Will We Look For?	What Will Be Measured?	How Will It Be Measured?
Establishment of university-community relationships	Number of community partners; duration of partnerships	Survey, interview
Involvement of community partners	Number of service-learning leaders designated by partners; perceptions regarding interaction between partners and institution	Survey, interview, focus group
Role of community partners	Contribution of community partners to program design and decision making	Survey, interview, focus group
Levels of university-community interaction	Institution's attention to community-identified priorities	Survey, interview, focus group
Capacity to meet unmet needs	Types of services provided; number of clients served	Survey, interview, focus group
Communication between partners and university	Nature of relationship; form and patterns of community involvement in university processes	Survey, interview, focus group, direct observation
Nature of partnership	Kind of activities	Interview, syllabus
Awareness of university	Knowledge of programs, activities	Interview, activity logs, focus group

Research Question 2

**How has the introduction of service-learning in medical education
affected the readiness of students for a career in the practice of medicine?**

Purpose:

To evaluate the effectiveness of service-learning as a developmental approach to preparing medical students for careers in the current policy, economic, social, and cultural environments of health-services delivery.

Phenomena to Be Studied:

Increase in students' knowledge of community health issues, level of involvement in service-learning, and personal capacity for service:
- knowledge of community needs assessment
- knowledge of barriers to health care
- knowledge of socioeconomic, environmental, and cultural determinants of health and illness
- understanding of distinction between service-learning and experiential clinical training
- service-learning leadership roles assumed by students
- intentions toward service following completion of program
- personal and professional development

What Will We Look For?	What Will Be Measured?	How Will It Be Measured?
Type and variety of student service-learning activity	Content of service-learning activities	Survey, interview, syllabus review
Awareness of community needs	Knowledge of community conditions and characteristics	Survey, interview, focus group, journal
Understanding of health policy and its implications	Understanding of local health policy and its impacts; linkage of experience to academic learning and content	Survey, interview, focus group, journal
Awareness of socioeconomic, environmental, and cultural determinants of health	Perception of unmet health needs; changes in awareness of links between community characteristics and health	Survey, interview, focus group, journal
Development of leadership skills	Attitude toward involvement	Survey, interview, focus group, direct observation
Commitment to service	Level of participation over time; plans for future service	Survey, interview, focus group, journal
Career choice (specialization)	Influence of service-learning on career plans	Survey, interview, journal
Sensitivity to diversity	Quality of student-community interactions; attitude toward community; reaction to clients with low health knowledge	Survey, interview, focus group, direct observation, journal
Involvement with community	Quality/quantity of interactions; attitudes toward involvement	Survey, interview, focus group, journal
Personal and professional development	Changes in awareness of personal capacity, communication skills, self-confidence	Interview, focus group, journal

Research Question 3

To what extent have faculty embraced service-learning as an integral part of the mission of medical education?

Purpose:
 To ascertain the level of commitment of faculty to the inclusion of service-learning in medical education.

Phenomena to Be Studied:
 Incorporation of service-learning into curriculum and professional pursuits:
- integration of service-learning activities into required curriculum
- understanding of distinction between service-learning and experiential clinical training
- expanding scholarly work to include a service-learning component
- leadership roles assumed by faculty
- knowledge of and commitment to community

What Will We Look For?	What Will Be Measured?	How Will It Be Measured?
Role in service-learning implementation	Number of faculty implementing service-learning; number of courses with service-learning component	Survey, syllabus analysis
Understanding of community needs	Ability to characterize community conditions and needs	Survey, interview, focus group
Awareness of socioeconomic, environmental, and cultural determinants of health	Perception of unmet health needs; changes in awareness of links between community characteristics and health	Survey, interview, focus group, journal
Development of leadership skills	Perceptions of role as a service-learning facilitator	Survey, interview, focus group, direct observation
Commitment to service	Attitude toward involvement; level of participation over time; plans for future service	Survey, interview, focus group, journal, vita
Sustained and expanding engagement in service-learning	Placement of service-learning in curriculum over time (introductory, advanced, etc.); integration of service-learning into other course components	Survey, interview, focus group, syllabus analysis
Nature of faculty/student interaction	Time spent on service-learning components; student mentoring	Survey, interview, focus group, direct observation
Nature of faculty/community interaction	Relationship to community partners	Survey, interview, focus group, direct observation
Scholarly interest in service-learning	Influence of service-learning on articles, presentations, committee/conference participation, grant proposals	Survey, interview, vita
Value placed on service-learning	Ability to distinguish between service-learning and clinical experience	Survey, interview, focus group, journal
Understanding of barriers to community health*N*services delivery	Knowledge of community history, strengths, problems	Survey, interview, focus group
Teaching methods and skills	Use of methods; implementation of new methods	Interview, direct observation, journal
Professional development	Attendance at seminars, workshops, etc.	
Interview, journal, vita		

Research Question 4

How has the institution's capacity to support service-learning in medical education changed?

Purpose:
> To establish the extent to which an institution is involved in service-learning activities and the factors that contribute to sustained commitment.

Phenomena to Be Studied:
> Broadening scope of institutional mission to include service-learning:
> - involvement in national service-learning networks
> - establishment of service-learning infrastructure
> - extent to which barriers to service-learning have been addressed
> - integration of service-learning activities into required curriculum

What Will We Look For?	What Will Be Measured?	How Will It Be Measured?
Departmental involvement	Number of faculty involved in service-learning coursework; establishment of departmental agenda for service	Survey, focus group
Commitment among academic leadership	Pattern of recognition/rewards; involvement in national service-learning network	Survey, interview
Investment of resources in support of service-learning	Evidence of investment in organizational infrastructure to support service-learning; investment in faculty development related to service-learning	Survey, interview
Image in community	Nature of institution/community communications; role and scope of community-university service-learning advisory group; perception of contribution of service-learning to meeting unmet needs; media coverage	Survey, interview, focus group, institutional records
Overall orientation to teaching and learning	Focus/content of professional development activities; number of faculty involved in service-learning; focus/content of dissertations and other major student projects	Survey, interview, analysis of records
Relationship of service-learning to clinical training	Nature of service-learning activities integrated into required curriculum	Survey, interview, focus group
Commitment to service-learning outside of health professions education (HPE)	Number of non-HPE faculty involved in service-learning coursework; relationships with other academic departments or institutions regarding service-learning	Survey, interview, focus group
Resource acquisition	Contribution levels; targeted proposals; awards for service	Survey, interview, institutional reports

Research Question 5

What impact does service-learning in medical education have on the participating community partners?

Purpose:

To determine the effect of partnership with the institution and attendant service-learning activities on community partners.

Phenomena to Be Studied:

Improvements in community service:
- extent to which unmet health needs have been addressed
- economic benefits
- social benefits

What Will We Look For?	What Will Be Measured?	How Will It Be Measured?
Establishment of ongoing relationships	Number and duration of partnerships	Survey, interview, focus group
Changing perceptions of unmet needs	Changes in goals of service-learning activities; changes in overall program structure and function	Interview
Capacity to serve community	Number of clients served; number of students involved; variety of activities	Survey, interview
Economic benefits	Cost of services provided by faculty/students; funding opportunities	Survey, interview
Social benefits	New connections/networks; increase in level of voluntarism	Survey, interview, focus group
Sensitivity to diversity	Comparison of partners' descriptions of community health concerns/needs	Interview, focus group
Nature, extent, and variety of partnerships	Level of community participation in service-learning advisory groups	Interview, focus group
Satisfaction with partnership	Changes in partner relationships; willingness to give both positive and negative feedback	Survey, interview, focus group
Community's sense of participation	Level of community-faculty-institution communication; changes in self-image, confidence, and knowledge of service-learning programs; willingness to participate in evaluation activities	Survey, interview, focus group
New insights about operations/activities	Changes in goals, activities, operations	Interview
Identification of future staff	Actual hiring	Survey, interview

Collecting data to respond to this model can provide a rich store of information on service-learning in medical education. These data can be presented in the context of describing the impact of service-learning on medical students, faculty, communities, and schools, and can also be formulated as comprehensive case studies of individual service-learning experiences (such as by course or defined academic learning experience). The findings can be used to inform the design and development of future service-learning experiences, provide input into curricular revision, and begin the process of documenting mission-based activities of medical schools and their parent institutions.

Such a broad range of variables, indicators, and appropriate measurement tools and approaches demands a blend of quantitative and qualitative approaches. We have identified a number of qualitative and quantitative methods for data collection that can be used independently or in combination, depending on individual information needs. Some of these approaches can be used in a pre-post format, others can be used for ongoing assessment throughout a course, and still others can be used for a one-time measurement. An overview of the indicators and appropriate measurement tools reveals three major categories of mechanisms or data-collection procedures: (1) in-person assessment; (2) independent reflection measures; and (3) review of existing documentation. The in-person methods include interviews of students, faculty, administrative leadership, and community representatives; focus groups conducted with students, course/program directors, faculty, and community partners; and direct observations of faculty, students, and community partners in the context of service-learning both in the classroom and in the community. The independent reflection measures are intended to capture reflections of faculty and students through personal journals, and through surveys of students, faculty, administrative leadership, and community representatives. The review of existing documentation can include analysis of syllabi, review of faculty vitae, analysis of existing institutional reports (admissions data, alumnae surveys, etc.), and activity/contact logs.

The number of methods used will be dictated by the resources available for such study; the specific methods will then dictate the nature of analytic methods. Our experience to date with both general education and the HPSISN program has provided a rich fund of information, offering extensive opportunities for approaches to analysis and synthesis.

Findings From Other Applications

In our pilot evaluation work at Portland State University, we set out to test a number of potential assessment strategies and approaches in order to develop a more refined and specific approach to measuring the impact of community-based teaching and learning. Methods such as surveys are relatively easy to design, administer, and analyze, yet the richest descriptive data may come from more time-intensive methods such as interviews and focus groups. Observations of classroom and community interactions are particularly informative yet very time-consuming, and require careful attention to ensure the validity of observations. While review of documentation such as syllabi and curricula vitae has much to offer potentially, these documents are often found to be less descriptive than might be hoped for. In order to rely upon them, it may be necessary to provide in advance guidelines for preparation so that the desired information will be included. Documents of this nature are probably most valuable for tracking change over a long period of time. Evaluation results have demonstrated the potential of service-learning for linking the teaching, research, and service roles of faculty — an outcome reflected in efforts to revise promotion and tenure guidelines and associated evaluation and reward systems.

In the process of data collection, it became apparent that most assessment strategies seemed to document impact on the four key constituencies as well as provide evaluative feedback for the continuous improvement of relevant courses. Our classroom observations began to suggest in some cases a nontraditional teaching paradigm. Faculty and student reflections offered in interviews and focus groups affirmed the value of service-learning. These general trends were immediately obvious in the process of collecting data.

A mechanism we have found particularly useful in assessing how service-learning changes the nature of the learning experience for both students and faculty involves a series of judgments along two continua adopted from Howard (1993). A continuum of teaching/learning contexts can be assessed from five perspectives:

• Whether commitment to other learners on the part of all participants moves from low to high;

• Whether the student role in learning moves from passive to active;

• Whether the faculty member's role in learning shifts from being directive to being facilitative;

• Whether learning orientation for both students and faculty evolves from an exclusively individual focus to a collective perspective that also considers the needs of the organization and the community; and

• Whether the overall pedagogical strategy moves from a "banking" approach where the faculty member deposits ideas into the students' heads to a "constructivist" approach that enables students to contribute to the knowledge base and build learning opportunities with other students and faculty members.

Shifts along these perspectives of the teaching/learning continuum serve to indicate movement from an *instruction* paradigm to a more *participatory learning* paradigm (Barr and Tagg 1995).

A second continuum assists in tracking the transition, if any, from traditional academic characteristics as represented on the continuum of teaching and learning qualities to more complex characteristics:

- Moving from theory to theory and experience;
- A shift in roles from the student as spectator to the student as participant, from the faculty member as teacher to the faculty member as teacher and learner, from the student as learner to student as learner and teacher;
- Emphasis on shared control, rather than faculty control, and on collective learning rather than individual learning;
- Moving from a clear distinction between teacher and learner to a blurring of this distinction;
- Recognizing ignorance as a resource, rather than avoiding it;
- Focusing on student and community needs rather than exclusively on student needs.

These continua reflect the academic underpinning of the learning experience, issues concerning the role of the student and that of the faculty member, and general orientations related to methods and applications of learning. It is anticipated that community-based learning will facilitate movement along each of these continua.

Applications in Medical Education

Early observations from the demonstration sites participating in the HPSISN program reveal both the great potential for service-learning in medical education and some of the difficulties inherent in such an undertaking. "Service-learning" seems to be a difficult concept for some educators to put in place: They understand service, and they understand learning, and they therefore assume that service-learning refers to an experience where learning includes providing service while learning about the nature of service. What may be missing in some situations is the mutuality of need reflected in the community-academy partnership, the drive for a community definition of needs, and an opportunity for reflection that enables students to process their experiences in the community and relate them to their professional training and personal development.

Another challenge lies in the creation of service-learning experiences that also engage other disciplines. Although much health professions practice is interdisciplinary, the challenges of creating interdisciplinary learning experiences as part of the required curriculum are incredible, given issues of scheduling, entrenched teaching methods, allocation of credit hours and tuition, and other structural factors (Headrick et al. 1995). Service-learning by medical students alone in a setting where they could better meet community needs through interdisciplinary experiences may be self-defeating — but at the same time, many would argue that any service-learning experience is better than none at all. These challenges of interdisciplinary education go far beyond the concept of service-learning, but may become more acute when community issues are included.

Finally, many medical educators may not see the need to devote curricular time to the development of community responsibility and an ethic of citizenship, given the demands of "pure" clinical experiences. Some educators assume that the quality of health services provided will be compromised in a community setting that may not be as well-resourced as traditional clinical settings. However, many providers will ultimately spend at least some time working in settings that do not have the "latest" in resources, and it is imperative that students learn how to be flexible and adaptive while they are still in their active professional-preparation mode. If community service experiences are viewed as "soft," it will be necessary to enlist vocal and influential champions who can stress the importance of these experiences in contributing to the preparation of future physicians.

Recommendations for Building, Evaluating, and Sustaining Service-Learning Programs

Experience to date suggests a number of recommendations for building, evaluating, and sustaining service-learning programs in medical education:

- **Engage a champion; leadership is crucial as well as passion**. There must be champions for service-learning as well as for assessment. It is vital to ensure representation of service-learning advocates on the medical school curriculum committee, as well as in the dean's decision-making circles, in seeking to achieve broad implementation across the school. Linking service-learning to curriculum goals, institutional mission, and professional development will signal institutional and college commitment to the concept. Champions must be articulate in answering questions about the impact of service-learning and therefore should be well-versed in relevant evaluation findings.

- **Do pilot tests when first implementing service-learning.** By starting small with a group of inquisitive faculty who are interested in studying their own teaching, as well as learning together, a medical school can test this pedagogic approach and seed several service-learning initiatives across the medical curriculum. Our initial invitation to PSU faculty to apply the assessment model to their courses received a positive response from faculty who were eager to participate in this pilot work. Courses were selected for participation based on a simple set of criteria that ensured a variety of representative academic programs, approaches, community partnerships, and class formats. Findings from the pilot tests will provide the groundwork for further institutionalization.

- **Offer incentives and rewards to those who participate.** Faculty respond to modest incentives to assist them to improve their teaching, in particular since most grant funding is based on biomedical or social research rather than on educational research. A small monetary incentive may be sufficient motivation for faculty to add service-learning components to their courses, or to adapt a community-based experiential learning opportunity to include service and reflection. Incentives and rewards acknowledge the value placed on curricular service-learning by the institution, and also signal an understanding of the level of effort given by faculty to organize these experience(s) and to participate in the assessment process. Faculty promotion and tenure guidelines may need to undergo revision to give increased value and recognition to community-based scholarship and related activities. Faculty will also feel rewarded if they are engaged in thoughtful discussions about the impact of service-learning and are encouraged to take an active role in the assessment and improvement of these experiences.

- **Obtain consent to engage in classroom research.** All students in selected courses need to be asked to participate, and should be given a voluntary informed-consent form to ensure their willingness to participate in this research. Similarly, representatives of the community involved in service-learning courses should also be informed of this research, and their consent should also be obtained.

- **Create a community advisory group.** Such a group brings faculty, students, academic leadership, and community representatives (both leaders and beneficiaries) together. It can contribute extensively to the delivery and interpretation of assessment outcomes. Community advisory groups have special value in assessing how well service-learning activities are addressing community needs.

- **Err on the side of collecting too much data.** The institutional investment in assessing service-learning will be justified when decision makers are provided with extensive information on the impact of these learning experiences. It is more advantageous to lean toward collecting more data, rather than less, particularly when the "extra" information is provided through interviews or focus groups and offers rich insights. While some aspects of impact can be quantified, the truly convincing arguments tend to relate to the personal stories and reflections of students, faculty, institutional leaders, and community partners. These reflections often highlight new insights and attitudes, and a new sense of community.

• **Create support structures.** To be truly successful in service-learning, a university's programs and infrastructure will need to reflect its commitment to community-university interaction through the adoption of new organizational strategies and support structures. Service-learning requires extra effort and is most successful when the university provides the support services needed to coordinate planning and evaluation, and to foster communication between the university and the community. Academic programs and curricula must reflect the needs not only of students but also of the surrounding community (or other identified service communities). Successful service-learning gives heed to community voices and responds to community priorities. The assessment model described here helps to capture these messages and to monitor impacts from the community's perspective. In this way, growing networks of university and community partners can realize the potential of supporting student access and success while enhancing community capacity.

• **Celebrate and share successes.** The enthusiasm generated through effective community-university partnerships and successful service-learning experiences is infectious, and should be shared with both participants and nonparticipants. Students and partners can be particularly effective in sharing lessons, accomplishments, new perspectives, challenges overcome, and opportunities for the future — all elements that can be identified by means of a comprehensive evaluation strategy. Feedback can then be used to plan subsequent service-learning experiences.

Many other recommendations could be made regarding building, sustaining, and evaluating service-learning. The points made here are intended as practical suggestions, relatively easy to implement and suitable for implementation in a medical education milieu.

Conclusions

Health professions educators take for granted the benefits of experiential learning; however, a focus on learning that incorporates a service commitment may seem unusual, despite the way in which it clearly responds to current policy initiatives within the health system. In 1993, the Pew Health Professions Commission recommended that health professions schools redefine their roles to better meet the needs of the emerging health-care system through the creation of new partnerships with health-care providers, payers, community-based organizations, and other constituencies (O'Neil 1993). Such partnerships have become increasingly visible on campuses across North America in the educational preparation of new health-care professionals.

The range of evaluative approaches presented in this chapter responds to concerns and questions about service-learning impacts, accommodates the range of constituencies influenced by service-learning, and seeks to address the paucity of approaches developed thus far for measuring service-learning outcomes. In addition, these approaches have the potential to support and inform institutional efforts to monitor the role of service-learning in the fulfillment of institutional mission.

Community-based learning is playing an increasingly important part in the educational preparation of medical students. It is quickly becoming a critical ingredient in their career expectations and in their preparation for environments created by managed care and community-oriented policies. We need the capability to test our assumptions about community-based learning, and to capture and measure its value-added benefits for all players, not just students. We need to be able to answer the question "How can we improve the educational experience?" and then be able to follow our answer with a justification of "how we know that a change is an improvement."

The multidimensional assessment of impact offered in this model can provide information to facilitate improvement, and the use of multiple measures and measurement tools is necessary to ensure the validity of the research and to provide richer information for future work. Measuring "impact" will build a body of evidence linking service-learning to professional success, professional development, and improved community-based health care. At the same time, it can help to improve institutional performance and program flexibility, guide the distribution and utilization of instructional resources, and perhaps encourage additional faculty to incorporate community-based teaching and learning into their academic agendas.

Service-learning offers a method for intensifying the socialization process for medical students by which they become more culturally sensitive, more aware of community concerns, and more conscious of a range of responses that will enable them, as practicing professionals, to participate more effectively in improving the health of their communities.

References

Barr, R.B., and J. Tagg. (November/December 1995). "From Teaching to Learning." *Change* 27(6): 12-25.

Driscoll, Amy, Barbara Holland, Sherril Gelmon, and Seanna Kerrigan. (Fall 1996). "An Assessment Model for Service-Learning: Comprehensive Case Studies of Impact on Faculty, Students, Community, and Institution." *Michigan Journal of Community Service Learning* 3: 66-71.

Eyler, Janet, and Dwight E. Giles. (1994). "Research and Evaluation in Community Service: The Higher Education Agenda." Proceedings from the Wingspread Service-Learning Conference, Racine, WI.

Gelmon, Sherril B., Amy Driscoll, Barbara Holland, and Seanna Kerrigan. (December 1995). "Community Impact of Experiential Learning: A Model for Assessment and Improvement." Paper presented at the First International Scientific Symposium on Improving Quality and Value in Health Care, Orlando, FL.

Gelmon, Sherril B., Barbara Holland, Seanna Kerrigan, and Amy Driscoll. (March 1996). "Assessing Community Impact of Service-Learning: Applications in the Health Professions." Paper presented at Community Partnerships in Health Professions Education: A National Conference on Service-Learning, Boston, MA.

Gelmon, Sherril B., Barbara Holland, and Beth Morris. (1996). "Health Professions Schools in Service to the Nation: Evaluation Prospectus." San Francisco, CA: UCSF Center for the Health Professions.

Gelmon, Sherril B., Sarena Seifer, Barbara Holland, and Kara Connors. (December 1996). "Improving Our Understanding of Community Impact: Assessing Service-Learning in the Health Professions." Paper presented at the Second International Scientific Symposium on Improving Quality and Value in Health Care, New Orleans, LA.

Giles, D.E., E. Honnet, and S. Migliore. (1991). "Setting the Agenda for Effective Research in Combining Service and Learning in the 1990s." Raleigh, NC: National Society of Experiential Education.

Headrick, Linda A., Linda Norman, Sherril B. Gelmon, and Marian Knapp. (1995). "Interdisciplinary Professional Education in the Continuous Improvement of Healthcare: The State of the Art." Rockville, MD: U.S. Department of Health and Human Services, Bureau of Health Professions.

Holland, Barbara, Sherril B. Gelmon, Amy Driscoll, and Seanna Kerrigan. (1996). "An Assessment Model for Service-Learning: Comprehensive Case Studies of the Impact on Faculty, Students, the Institution, and Community." Working paper. Portland, OR: Portland State University.

Howard, Jeffrey. (1993). "Community Service-Learning in the Curriculum." In *Praxis I: A Faculty Casebook on Community Service Learning,* edited by Joseph Galura and Jeffrey Howard, pp. 1-10. Ann Arbor, MI: OCSL Press.

Langley, J., Kevin Nolan, and Thomas Nolan. (1994). "The Foundation of Improvement." *Quality Progress* 12: 81-86.

O'Neil, Edward H. (1993). *Health Professions Education for the Future: Schools in Service to the Nation.* San Francisco, CA: Pew Health Professions Commission.

Ramaley, Judith A., president, Portland State University. (1996). Personal communication.

Appendix

Service-Learning Resources

Programs and Organizations

Health Professions Schools in Service to the Nation. The HPSISN program, its grantees' experiences, and the preliminary outcomes of its external evaluation are important resources to medical schools seeking to develop community partnerships and to integrate service-learning into their curriculum. The HPSISN program office, based at the Center for the Health Professions at the University of California–San Francisco, maintains a service-learning bibliography, grantee service-learning course descriptions, and other resource materials. For more information:
ph 415/502-4771, email *karac@itsa.ucsf.edu*
http://futurehealth.ucsf.edu/hpsisn.html

Campus-based centers. Many universities have campus-based centers for community service and service-learning. These centers are often based on the undergraduate campus and do not often have relationships with the university's health professions schools. The University of Utah's Bennion Center, University of Kentucky's Office of Experiential Education, Brown University's Swearer Center, and University of Washington's Carlson Center are examples of university-based centers that have established productive relationships with their medical schools. These centers can be wonderful sources of reference material on service-learning, faculty-development activities, and connections to faculty in other disciplines who are involved in service-learning and facilitators of community partnerships.

Community-Campus Partnerships for Health. A national nonprofit organization, Community-Campus Partnerships for Health fosters partnerships between communities and health professions schools, and serves as a national resource through its annual conferences, summer faculty institutes on service-learning, electronic discussion groups, publications, and custom-designed training and technical assistance programs. For more information:
ph 415/476-7081, email *ccph@itsa.ucsf.edu*
http://futurehealth.ucsf.edu/ccph.html

Campus Compact. Campus Compact is a national coalition of more than 520 college and university presidents established to create public-service opportunities for their students and develop an expectation of service as

an integral part of the undergraduate experience. More than a dozen states have affiliated state Campus Compacts, which often sponsor state-wide conferences, provide faculty development, publish resource guides, and offer other services to member institutions. For more information:
http://www.compact.org

National Society for Experiential Education. NSEE is a membership association and national resource center that promotes experience-based approaches to teaching and learning. NSEE sponsors national conferences, maintains a resource and consultant referral center, and publishes resource materials on experiential education and service-learning. For more information:
ph 919/787-3263, email *info@nsee.org*
http://www.nsee.org

Corporation for National Service. This federal agency supports service-learning in higher education through its Learn and Serve America: Higher Education grant program. In addition to supporting the HPSISN program, more than a dozen individual health professions schools have received service-learning grants from CNS. For more information:
ph 202/606-5000
http://www.cns.gov

Websites

Community-Campus Partnerships for Health
http://futurehealth.ucsf.edu/ccph.html

U.S. Department of Housing and Urban Development, Office of University Partnerships
http://oup.aspensys.com

Corporation for National Service (CNS)
http://www.cns.gov

CNS, Learn and Serve America: Higher Education
http://www.cns.gov/learn/html

U.S. Department of Education
http://www.ed.gov

Centers for Disease Control and Prevention
http://www.cdc.gov/

U.S. Department of Health and Human Services
http://www.os.dhhs.gov

Health Resources and Services Administration (HRSA)
http://www.hrsa.dhhs.gov

HRSA, Academic-Community Partnership Initiative
http://www/hrsa.gov/bhpr/hrsaacpi.htm

HRSA, Bureau of Health Professions
http://hrsa.dhhs.gov/bhpr

HRSA, Bureau of Primary Health Care
http://www.bphc.hrsa.dhhs.gov

International Healthy Cities Foundation
http://www.oneworld.org/cities/cities_info.html

Community Health Information Resources
http://www.chmis.org

Healthcare Forum
http://www.healthonline.com/thf.htm

Health Professions Schools in Service to the Nation
http://futurehealth.ucsf.edu/hpsisn.html

Service-Learning Homepage
http://csf.colorado.edu/sl

Association for Experiential Education
http://www.princeton.edu/~rcurtis/aee.html

National Service-Learning Cooperative Clearinghouse
http://www.nicsl.coled.umn.edu/otherweb.html

National Service Resource Center
http://www.etr-associates.org/NSRC

ERIC Clearinghouse on Higher Education
http://www.gwu.edu/~eriche

National Society for Experiential Education
http://www.nsee.org

Partnership for Service-Learning
http://studyabroad.com/psl/

Campus Compact National Center for Community Colleges
http://www.mc.maricopa.edu/academic/compact

Campus Compact
http://www.compact.org

Campus Outreach Opportunity League
http://www.cool2serve.org/cool/home.html

Center for the Health Professions,
at University of California–San Francisco
http://futurehealth.ucsf.edu

Breakaway Alternative Break Community Service
http://www.vanderbilt.edu/breakaway

Network of Community-Oriented Educational Institutions
for the Health Sciences
http://www.unimaas.nl/~network/welcome.htm

Albert Schweitzer Fellowship
http://www.healthnet.org/schweitzer

National Fund for Medical Education
http://futurehealth.ucsf.edu/nfme.html

Publications

The following publications provide direction and useful information for developing service-learning programs. Please note that some publications are listed with telephone or contact information for ordering a particular book or article. The list is not intended to be exhaustive but reflects a compilation of materials recommended by the monograph coeditors.

Community Building

Coles, Robert. (1993). *The Call of Service*. New York, NY: Houghton Mifflin.

Handler, A., et al. (1994). "Building Bridges Between Schools of Public Health and Public Health Practice." *American Journal of Public Health* 84(7): 1077-1080.

Kretzmann, John, and John McKnight. (1993). *Building Communities From the Inside Out*. Evanston, IL: Northwestern University, Center for Urban Affairs and Policy Research. (800/331-3761)

Lappe, Frances Moore, and Paul Martin DuBois. (1994). *The Quickening of America: Rebuilding Our Nation, Remaking Our Lives*. San Francisco, CA: Jossey-Bass. (415/433-1740)

McKnight, John. (1990). *The Careless Society: Community and Its Counterfeits*. Evanston, IL: Northwestern University, Center for Urban Affairs and Policy Research. (800/331-3761)

Community-Campus Partnerships

Foreman, S. (1994). "Social Responsibility and the Academic Medical Center: Building Community-Based Systems for the Nation's Health." *Academic Medicine* 69(2): 97-102.

Journal of Public Service and Outreach. To order, contact Albert F. Ike, managing editor, ph 706/542-6167, fax 706/542-6278, email *jpso@uga.cc.uga.edu*. This journal also welcomes submission of research. For more information, contact Donna Butler, coeditor, ph 706/542-4051, fax 706/542-4051, email *dqbutler@coe.uga.edu*.

Maurana, C.A., and K. Goldenberg. (1996). "A Successful Academic-Community Partnership to Improve the Public's Health." *Academic Medicine* 71(5): 425-431.

Nora, L.M., S.R. Daugherty, A. Mattis-Peterson, L. Stevenson, and L.J. Goodman. (1994). "Improving Cross-Cultural Skills of Medical Students Through Medical School–Community Partnerships." *Western Journal of Medicine* 161(2): P144-P147.

Richards, Ronald, ed. (1995). *Building Partnerships: Educating Health Profession-als for the Communities They Serve.* San Francisco, CA: Jossey-Bass. (415/433-1740)

Skelton, W. Douglas, and Marian Osterweis. (1993). *Promoting Community Health: The Role of the Academic Health Center.* Washington, DC: Association of Academic Health Centers. (202/265-9600)

Smego, R.A., and J. Costante. (1996). "An Academic Health Center–Commu-nity Partnership: The Morgantown Health Right Free Clinic." *Academic Medi-cine* 71(6): 613-621.

Community Sites for Health Professions Education

Barger, S.E., and P.M. Kline. (1993). "Community Health-Service Programs in Academe: Unique Learning Opportunities for Students." *Nurse Educator* 18(6): 22-26.

Hedgecock, J., M. Castro, and W.B. Cruikshank. (1992). "Community Health Centers: A Resource for Service and Training." *Henry Ford Hospital Medical Journal* 40(1-2): 45-49.

National Association of Community Health Centers. (1994). *TEACH: Teaching for Essential Access to Community Health. A Practical Guide for Teaching Commu-nity Health Centers.* Washington, DC: NACHC.

Zuvekas, A., and S. Rosenbaum. (1995). *Teaching Community Health Centers: A Guide.* Washington, DC: National Association of Community Health Cen-ters.

Cultural Competence

Anderson, P.P., and E.S. Fenichel. (1989). *Serving Culturally Diverse Families of Infants and Toddlers With Disabilities.* Washington, DC: National Center for Clinical Infant Programs.

Barker, J.C. (September 1992). "Cultural Diversity: Changing the Context of Medical Practice." *Western Journal of Medicine* 157(3): 248-254.

Braithwaite, L.B., and N. Lythcott. (January 13, 1989). "Community Empow-erment as a Strategy for Health Promotion for Blacks and Other Minority Populations." *Journal of the American Medical Association* 261(2): 282-283.

Couto, Richard. (1991). *Ain't Gonna Let Nobody Turn Me Round: The Pursuit of Racial Justice in the Rural South*. Philadelphia, PA: Temple University Press.

National Civic Review. (1992). *The Diverse Society* 81(3). (800/223-6004)

Nora, L.M., S.R. Daugherty, A. Mattis-Peterson, L. Stevenson, and L.J. Goodman. (1994). "Improving Cross-Cultural Skills of Medical Students Through Medical School–Community Partnerships." *Western Journal of Medicine* 161(2): 144-147.

Scott, Joan, and Amy Holmes. (1993). *Discovering Each Other: A Cross-Cultural Service-Learning Experience With Mexican-American Migrant Farm Workers*. Ann Arbor, MI: University of Michigan, OCSL Press. (313/763-3548)

Ventres, W., and P. Gordon. (1990). "Communication Strategies in Caring for the Underserved." *Journal of Health Care for the Poor and Underserved* 1(3): 305-314.

Curriculum Development

Buchen, I. (January 1995). "Service-Learning and Curriculum Transfusion." *NASSP Bulletin* 79: 66-70.

Hammers, P.S. (April 1985). "Experiential-Based Learning vs. Lecture-Based Learning." *Journal of Business Education* 60(7): 283-287.

Jackson, K., ed. (in press). *Redesigning Curricula: Models of Service-Learning Syllabi*. Providence, RI: Campus Compact.

Evaluation Findings

Bringle, R.G., and J.F. Kremer. (1993). "An Evaluation of an Intergenerational Service-Learning Project for Undergraduates." *Educational Gerontologist* 19: 407-416.

Brooks, C.H. (1992). "Do Area Health Education Center Programs Produce Primary Care Specialists? Results of a Longitudinal Study." *International Journal of Health Services* 22(3): P567-578.

Denice, S., et al. (February 1996). "Community-Oriented Dental Education: Student Perceptions, Baseline to Year One." Abstract presentation at the 73rd Annual Session and Exposition, American Association of Dental Schools, Washington, DC.

Giles, D., and J. Eyler. (1994). "The Impact of a College Community Service Laboratory on Students' Personal, Social, and Cognitive Outcomes." *Journal of Adolescence* 7: 325-339.

Grum, C.M., et al. (1996). "Consequences of Shifting Medical Student Education to the Outpatient Setting: Effects on Performance and Experiences." *Academic Medicine* 71(1S): S99-S101.

Hesser, G. (1995). "Faculty Assessment of Student Learning: Outcomes Attributed to Service-Learning and Evidence of Changes in Faculty Attitudes About Experiential Education." *Michigan Journal of Community Service Learning* 2: 33-42.

Konene, J.C., et al. (1992). "Evaluations of Three Graduating Classes of a Required Community Health Project." *Academic Medicine* 67(7): 479-481.

Krackov, S.K. (1982). "Influence of Site on Ambulatory Care Residency Education in Internal Medicine." PhD dissertation, University of Rochester.

Kurlandsky, L.E., M. Potts, and A. Kumar. (April 1994). "Pediatric Clerkship Performance in Diverse Community Clinical Settings." *Pediatrics* 93(4): 608-610.

Markus, G.B., et al. (1993). "Integrating Community Service and Classroom Instruction Enhances Learning: Results From an Experiment." *Educational Evaluation and Policy Analysis* 15: 410-419.

Mennin, S.P., et al. (1996). "A Survey of Graduates in Practice From the University of New Mexico's Conventional and Community-Oriented, Problem-Based Tracks." *Academic Medicine* 71(10): 1079-1089.

Plake, K.S., and A.P. Wolfgang. (Spring 1996). "Impact of Experiential Education on Pharmacy Students' Perceptions of Health Roles." *American Journal of Pharmaceutical Education* 60(1): 13-19.

Rolfe, I.E., S.A. Pearson, and L. Barnsley. (1996). "Attitudes of Doctors Toward Community Medicine: Differences Between Graduates From Innovative and Traditional Medical Schools." *Teaching and Learning in Medicine* 8(2): 77-82.

Satran, L., I.B. Harris, S. Allen, D.C. Anderson, G.A. Poland, and W.L. Miller. (May 1993). "Hospital-Based Versus Community-Based Clinical Education: Comparing Performances and Course Evaluations by Students in Their Second-Year Pediatrics Rotation." *Academic Medicine* 68(5): 380-382.

Shore, W.B., and J.E. Rodnick. (1993). "A Required Fourth-Year Ambulatory Clerkship: A 10-Year Experience With Family Practice and Primary Care Internal Medicine Sites." *Family Medicine* 25: 34-40.

Wechsler, A., and J. Fogel. (1995). "The Outcomes of a Service-Learning Program." *National Quarterly of the Society for Experiential Education* 20(4): 6-7, 25-26.

Wilson, S.R., and V.K. Fowkes. (January 1990). *Evaluation of the Impact of the National Area Health Education Center Program.* HRSA Contract No. 240-88-0031. Palo Alto, CA: American Institutes for Research.

Evaluation Methods

Exley, R.J., S. Johnson, and D. Johnson. (1996). "Assessing the Effectiveness of Service-Learning." In *Expanding Boundaries: Serving and Learning,* edited by J. Raybuck, pp. 62-63. Washington, DC: Corporation for National Service. (202/606-5000 x117)

Friedman, C.P., et al. (1990). "Charting the Winds of Change: Evaluating Innovative Medical Curricula." *Academic Medicine* 65: 8-14.

Illinois Campus Compact. (1996). *Attitude Assessment Survey: A Guidebook and Assessment Tool to Measure a Developing Sense of Social Responsibility and Personal Growth Through Community Service.* (309/438-8123)

Krueger, R.A. (1988). *Focus Groups: A Practical Guide for Applied Research.* Newbury Park, CA: Sage Publications.

McMaster University. (1996). *Evaluation Methods: A Resource Handbook.* Program for Educational Development, Program for Faculty Development. (905/525-9140 x23114)

Morgan, D.L. (1993). *Successful Focus Groups: Advancing the State of the Art.* Newbury Park, CA: Sage Publications.

Morris, Lynn Lyons, and Carol Taylor Fitz-Gibbon. (1987). *Evaluator's Handbook.* Newbury Park, CA: Sage Publications.

———. (1987). *How to Assess Program Implementation.* Newbury Park, CA: Sage Publications.

———. (1987). *How to Communicate Evaluation Findings.* Newbury Park, CA: Sage Publications.

———. (1987). *How to Design a Program Evaluation.* Newbury Park, CA: Sage Publications.

———. (1987). *How to Measure Attitudes.* Newbury Park, CA: Sage Publications.

———. (1987). *How to Measure Performance and Use Tests.* Newbury Park, CA: Sage Publications.

Schmiede, A. (1994). *Focus Group Guidelines: FIPSE Service-Learning Project.* Nashville, TN: Vanderbilt University.

Faculty Development

Bland, C.J., F.T. Stritter, C.C. Schmitz, J.A. Aluise, and R.A. Henry. (June 1988). "Project to Identify Essential Faculty Skills and Develop Model Curricula for Faculty Development Programs." *Journal of Medical Education* 63: 467-469.

DeWitt, T.G., R.L. Goldberg, and K.B. Roberts. (January 1993). "Developing Community Faculty: Principles, Practice, and Evaluation." *American Journal of Diseases of Children* 147: 49-53.

Fulkerson, P.K., and R. Wang-Cheng. (1997). "Community-Based Faculty: Motivation and Rewards." *Family Medicine* 29(2): 105-107.

Galura, Joseph, Rachel Meiland, and Randy Ross. (1993). *Praxis I: A Faculty Casebook on Community Service Learning.* Ann Arbor, MI: OCSL Press. (313/763-3548)

———— . (1993). *Praxis II: Service-Learning Resources for University Students, Staff, and Faculty.* Ann Arbor, MI: OCSL Press. (313/763-3548)

Stanton, Timothy. (Fall 1994). "The Experience of Faculty Participants in an Instructional Development Seminar on Service-Learning." *Michigan Journal of Community Service Learning* 1(1): 7-20.

Usatine, R.P., C.S. Hodgson, E.T. Marshall, D.W. Whitman, S.J. Slavin, and M.S. Wilkes. (October 1995). "Reactions of Family Medicine Community Preceptors to Teaching Medical Students." *Family Medicine* 27(9): 566-570.

Health Professions Education

American Medical Student Association/Foundation. (1995). *National Health Service Corps Educational Program for Clinical and Community Issues in Primary Care.* (703/620-6600).

American Public Health Association. (1991). *Healthy Communities 2000: Model Standards.* Washington, DC: APHA.

Area Health Education Center. (Spring 1995). *From the Ground Up! A Workbook on Coalition Building and Community Development.* (413/253-4283).

Bellack, J. (1996). "Education for the Community." *Journal of Nursing Education* 34(8): 342-343.

Bhattacharji, S., A. Joseph, S. Abraham, J. Muliyil, K.R. John, and N. Ethirajan. (January 1990). "Teaching Nutrition to Medical Students: A Community-Based Problem-Solving Approach." *Medical Education* 24(1): 32-36.

Boelen, C. (1992). "Medical Education Reform: The Need for Global Action." *Academic Medicine* 11: 745-749.

Carlos, W., et al. (1996). "UTHSCA Dental Van Program: Teaching Initiatives Promoting Access to Dental Care." Abstract presented at the 73rd Annual Session and Exposition of the American Association of Dental Schools, Washington, DC.

Committee for the Study of the Future of Public Health, Institute of Medicine. (1988). *Future of Public Health.* Washington, DC: National Academy Press.

Desjardins, P. (1996). "Creating a Community-Oriented Curriculum and Culture: Lessons Learned From the 1993-1996 Ongoing New Jersey Experiment." *Journal of Dental Education* 60(10): 821-826.

Faller, H.S., et al. (1996). "Bridge to the Future: Nontraditional Clinical Settings, Concepts, and Issues." *Journal of Nursing Education* 34(8): 344-349.

Field, M.J., ed. (1995). *Dental Education at the Crossroads*. Washington, DC: National Academy Press.

Fournier, A.M., A. Perez-Stable, and P.J. Greer, Jr. (December 8, 1993). "Lessons From a Clinic for the Homeless: The Camillus Health Concern." *Journal of the American Medical Association* 270(22): 2721-2724.

Glasser, M., and J. Gravdal. (1987). "Graduates' Assessment of Undergraduate Training in Ambulatory Primary Care Education." *Journal of Medical Education* 62: 386-393.

Greer, T., et al. (1993). "A Comparison of Student Clerkship Experiences in Community Practices and Residency-Based Clinics." *Family Medicine* 25: 322-326.

Hale, F.A., et al. (1992). *The Family-Practice Residency Community/Migrant Health Center Linkage Manual*. Kansas City, MO: American Academy of Family Physicians.

Hamad, B. (January 1991). "Community-Oriented Medical Education: What Is It?" *Medical Education* 25(1): P16-P22.

Kaufman, A. (1990). "Rurally Based Education: Confronting Social Forces Underlying Ill Health." *Academic Medicine* 65(3S): S18-S21.

Klevens, J., et al. (1992). "Teaching Community-Oriented Primary Care in a Traditional Medical School: A Two Year Progress Report." *Journal of Community Health* 17(4): 231-245.

Nutting, P.A. (1987). *Community Oriented Primary Care: From Principles to Practice*. Publication No. HRSA-PE 86-1. Washington, DC: U.S. Department of Health and Human Services, Public Health Service.

O'Neil, E.H. (1993). *Health Professions Education for the Future: Schools in Service to the Nation.* San Francisco, CA: Pew Health Professions Commission. (415/476-8181)

————, and S.D. Seifer. (January 1995). "The Impact of Health Reform on Medical Education: Forces Toward Generalism." *Academic Medicine* 70 (1 Suppl): S37-S43.

Pew Health Professions Commission. (1995). *Health Professions Education for the Future: Schools in Service to the Nation.* San Francisco, CA: Pew Health Professions Commission. (415/476-8181)

Public Health Service. (1991). *Healthy People 2000.* Publication No. PHS 91-50213. Washington, DC: U.S. Department of Health and Human Services, Public Health Service.

Reinsmith, W.A. (1987). "Philosophy and Values for Pharmacy Students: Attempting to Meet a Need." *American Journal of Pharmacy Education* 51: 153-159.

Romero, L., W.A. Heffron, and A. Kaufman. (January-February 1990). "The Educational Opportunities in a Departmental Program of Health Care for the Homeless." *Family Medicine* 22(1): 60-62.

Schmidt, H.G., et al. (1991). "Network of Community-Oriented Educational Institutions for the Health Sciences." *Academic Medicine* 66: 259-263.

Schroeder, S.A., and J.A. Showstack. (1989). "Academic Medicine as a Public Trust." *Journal of the American Medical Association* 262: 803-812.

Seifer, S.D., and E.H. O'Neil. (1995). "Medical Education's Response to Primary Care." In *Medicine and Health Care for the Twenty-First Century,* edited by D.B. Nash, pp. 146-172. Philadelphia, PA: Pennsylvania Academy of Science Press.

Steffee, C.H. (January 1994). "Sowing the Seeds of Primary Care Medicine: The Early Community Experience in Medical Education." *North Carolina Medical Journal* 55(1): P45-P46.

Stein, D.H., and M.E. Salive. (1996) "Adequacy of Training in Preventive Medicine and Public Health: A National Survey of Residency Graduates." *American Journal of Preventive Medicine* 71(4): 375-380.

Summerlin, H.H., Jr., S.E. Landis, and P.R. Olson. (February 1993). "A Community-Oriented Primary Care Experience for Medical Students and Family Practice Residents." *Family Medicine* 25(2): 95-99.

Thomas, S.G., A. Janer, and D.E. Beck. (Spring 1996). "A Continuous Community Pharmacy Practice Experience: Design and Evaluation of Instructional Materials." *American Journal of Pharmaceutical Education* 60(1): 4-12.

University of Texas–Houston, Health Policy Institute. (April 1996). "The Vision of Community-Oriented Primary Care." In *Community Oriented Primary Care: A Vision for Health.* Conference proceedings.

Institutional Change

Bok, D. (1982). *Beyond the Ivory Tower: Social Responsibilities of the Modern University.* Cambridge, MA: Harvard University Press.

Boyer, E.L. (1990). *Scholarship Reconsidered: Priorities of the Professoriate.* Princeton, NJ: Carnegie Foundation for the Advancement of Teaching.

Cisneros, H.G. (February 1995). *The University and the Urban Challenge.* Washington, DC: U.S. Department of Housing and Urban Development.

Dowling, N. (September 1986). *Motivation and the Role of Faculty in Public Service in the University of California.* (Available from University of Winnipeg, Institute of Urban Studies)

Faculty Rewards for Public Service Committee. (May 1983). *Report of the Subcommittee on Faculty Rewards for Public Service.* Davis, CA: University of California–Davis, Office of the Vice-Chancellor, Academic Affairs.

Kaufman, A., et al. (1989). "The New Mexico Experiment: Educational Innovation and Institutional Change." *Academic Medicine* 64: 285-294.

Kerr, C. (1963). *The Uses of the University.* New York, NY: Harper and Row.

Mayer, E. (1990). "Academic Support for Rural Practice: The Role of Area Health Education Centers in the School of Medicine." *Academic Medicine* 65(12): S45-S50.

Interdisciplinary Education

Astin, A.W. (September/October 1987). "Competition or Cooperation? Teaching Teamwork as a Basic Skill." *Change* 19(15): 12-19.

Connors, K., S. Seifer, J. Sebastian, D.C. Bramble, and R. Hart. (Fall 1996). "Interdisciplinary Collaboration in Service-Learning: Lessons From the Field." *Michigan Journal of Community Service Learning,* pp. 113-127.

Erskel, E.A., et al. (1996). "Intensive Rural Immersion of Nursing Students in Rural Interdisciplinary Care." *Journal of Nursing Education* 34(8): 359-365.

Grant, R.W., L.J. Finocchio, and the California Primary Care Consortium Subcommittee on Interdisciplinary Collaboration. (1995). *Interdisciplinary Collaborative Teams in Primary Care: A Model Curriculum and Resource Guide.* San Francisco, CA: Pew Health Professions Commission. (415/476-8181)

Hanley, M., and N. Gehrke. (1995). *Interprofessional Collaboration Resource Guide: A Resource Guide of Learning Activities.* Seattle, WA: University of Washington, Human Services Policy Center, Training for Interprofessional Collaboration Project. (206/685-3135)

Ivey, S.L., et al. (August 1988). "A Model for Teaching About Interdisciplinary Practice in Health Care Settings." *Journal of Allied Health* 17(3): 189-195.

Knapp, M.S. (1997). *Preparing to Collaborate: Interprofessional Education Through University-Community Partnerships.* Seattle, WA: University of Washington, Human Services Policy Center, Training for Interprofessional Collaboration Project. (206/685-3135)

Moulder, P.A., A.M. Staal, and M. Grant. (November-December 1988). "Making the Interdisciplinary Team Work." *Rehabilitation Nursing* 13(6): 338-339.

"The Pharmacist as a Member of the Primary Care Team: Experience in a University-Based Program." (January 1982). *Postgraduate Medicine* 71(1): 97-102.

Riley, K., W. Myers, M.J. Gordon, M. Laskowski, S. Kriebel, and S. Dobie. (December 1991). "A Collaborative Approach to a Primary Care Preclinical Preceptorship for Underserved Settings." *Academic Medicine* 66(12): 776-777.

Slack, M.K., and M.M. McEwan. (1993). "Pharmacy Student Participation in Interdisciplinary Community-Based Training." *American Journal of Pharmaceutical Education* 57(3): 251-257.

Zungalo, E. (1994). "Interdisciplinary Education in Primary Care: The Challenge." *Nursing and Health Care* 15(6): 288-292.

Reflection

Eyler, J., D. Giles, and A. Schmiede. (1996). *A Practitioner's Guide to Reflection in Service-Learning: Student Voices and Reflections.* Nashville, TN: Vanderbilt University.

Florida Campus Compact. (1995). *The Tackle Box. Fishing for How-to-Do-It Tools: Reflection.* (407/632-1111)

Kitchener, Karen, and Patricia King. (1994). *Developing Reflective Judgement.* San Francisco, CA: Jossey-Bass. (415/733-1740)

Schön, Donald. (1987). *Educating the Reflective Practitioner.* San Francisco, CA: Jossey-Bass. (415/433-1740)

Service-Learning

Albert, Gail. (1994). *Service-Learning Reader: Reflections and Perspectives on Service.* Raleigh, NC: National Society for Experiential Education. (919/787-3263)

Cha, S., and M. Rothman. (1994). *Service Matters: A Sourcebook for Community Service in Higher Education.* Providence, RI: Campus Compact.

Colby, Anne, and William Damon. (1992). *Some Do Care: Contemporary Lives of Moral Commitment.* New York, NY: Free Press.

Foundation for Long-Term Care. (1996). *Service-Learning in Elder Care.* (To order, send $12.00 to Foundation for Long-Term Care, 150 State Street, Suite 301, Albany, NY 12207-1698, ph 518/449-7873, fax 518/455-8908, email carol@nyahsa.org)

Freire, Paulo. (1970). *Pedagogy of the Oppressed.* New York, NY: Herder and Herder.

Furco, A. (1996). "Service-Learning: A Balanced Approach to Experiential Education." In *Expanding Boundaries: Serving and Learning,* edited by B. Taylor, pp. 2-6. Washington, DC: Corporation for National Service. (202/606-5000 x117)

Honnet, E.P., and S.J. Poulsen, eds. (1989). *Principles of Good Practice for Combining Service and Learning.* Racine, WI: The Johnson Foundation.

Innovative Democratic Education and Learning Through Service. (1992). Alexandria, VA: National Association of Partners in Education, Inc. (703/836-4880)

Jacoby, Barbara, et al. (1996). *Service-Learning in Higher Education: Concepts and Practices.* San Francisco, CA: Jossey-Bass. (415/433-1740)

Kendall, Jane, and Associates, eds. (1990). *Combining Service and Learning: A Resource Book for Community and Public Service.* Vols. 1 and 2. Raleigh, NC: National Society for Internships and Experiential Education. (919/787-3263)

Kolb, D.A. (1984). *Experiential Learning: Experience as the Source of Learning and Development.* Englewood Cliffs, NJ: Prentice-Hall.

Kraft, Richard, and Marc Swadener. (1994). *Building Community: Service Learning in the Academic Disciplines.* Denver, CO: Colorado Campus Compact. (303/620-4941)

Luce, Janet. (1988). *Combining Service and Learning: A Resource Book for Community and Public Service. Vol. 3, An Annotated Bibliography.* Raleigh, NC: National Society for Internships and Experiential Education. (919/787-3263)

Michigan Journal of Community Service Learning. Ann Arbor, MI: University of Michigan, OCSL Press. (Contact Jeff Howard, editor, ph 313/763-3548)

Seidman, A., and C. Temper. (1994). *Legal Issues for Service-Learning Programs.* Washington, DC: Non-Profit Risk Management Center. (202/785-3891)

Wolfe, M.K., and S.P. Gibson. (1996). "The Shriver Center Top Ten List of Strategies for a Successful Program." In *Expanding Boundaries: Serving and Learning,* edited by B. Taylor, pp. 44-45. Washington, DC: Corporation for National Service. (202/606-5000 x117)

Service-Learning in Health Professions Education

Cauley, K., C.A. Maurana, and M.A. Clark. (1996). "Service-Learning for Health Professions Students in the Community: Matching Enthusiasm, Talent, and Time With Experience, Real Need, and Schedules." In *Expanding Boundaries: Serving and Learning,* edited by B. Taylor, pp. 54-57. Washington, DC: Corporation for National Service. (202/606-5000 x117)

Couto, Richard. (1982). *Streams of Idealism and Health-Care Innovation.* New York, NY: Teachers College Press.

Gauthier, M.A., B. Kelley, and P. Matteson. (1996). "Introduction to the Community Through Sensory Information." In *Expanding Boundaries: Serving and Learning,* edited by B. Taylor, pp. 58-61. Washington, DC: Corporation for National Service. (202/606-5000 x117)

Seifer, S.D., K. Connors, and E.H. O'Neil. (1996). "Combining Service and Learning in Partnership With Communities." *Academic Medicine* 71(5): 527.

Seifer, S.D., S. Mutha, and K. Connors. (1996). "Service-Learning in Health Professions Education: Barriers, Facilitators, and Strategies for Success." In *Expanding Boundaries: Serving and Learning,* edited by B. Taylor, pp. 36-41. Washington, DC: Corporation for National Service. (202/606-5000 x117)

Zweifler, J. (May 1993). "Balancing Service and Education: Linking Community Health Centers and Family Practice Residency Programs." *Family Medicine* 25(5): 312-315.

Student Leadership

Association of American Medical Colleges. (1983). *Student Participation in Organizations and Institutional Policy Making.* Series in Academic Medicine. San Francisco, CA: Jossey-Bass. (415/433-1740)

Lempert, D. (1996). *Escape From the Ivory Tower: Student Adventures in Democratic Experiential Education.* San Francisco, CA: Jossey-Bass.

Meisel, W., and R. Hackett, eds. (1986). *Building a Movement: A Resource Book for Students in Community Service.* St. Paul, MN: Campus Outreach Opportunity League Press.

Serow, R. (Summer 1990). "Volunteering and Values: An Analysis of Students' Participating in Community Service." *Journal of Research and Development in Education* 23(4): 198-203.

——— , and J. Dreyden. (Fall 1990). "Community Service Among College and University Students: Individual and Institutional Relationships." *Adolescence* 25(99): 553-566.

Stanton, T., and K. Ali. (1987). *The Experienced Hand: A Student Manual for Making the Most of an Internship.* Cranston, RI: Carroll Press.

Wieckowski, T. (Spring 1992). "Student Community-Service Programs: The Academic Connection." *NASPA Journal* 29(3): 207-212.

Contributors to This Volume

Volume Editors

Sarena D. Seifer, MD, is executive director of Community-Campus Partnerships for Health, a research assistant professor in the Department of Health Services at the University of Washington School of Public Health and Community Medicine, and a senior fellow at the Center for the Health Professions, University of California-San Francisco.

Kris Hermanns, BA, EdM, is associate director of the Swearer Center for Public Service at Brown University.

Judy Lewis, MPhil, is director of community-based education and an associate professor in the Department of Community Medicine at the University of Connecticut School of Medicine.

Authors

Franklin R. Banks, PhD, is an associate professor in the Division of Health Behavior and Health Promotion, School of Public Health, at the Ohio State University.

Bonnie Beck, MPH, is a former CHAP (Community Health Advancement Program) educator in the Department of Family Medicine at the University of Washington.

Bruce Behringer, MPH, is director of the Office of Rural and Community Health at East Tennessee State University.

Bruce Bennard, PhD, is an evaluator for the Community Partnership Initiative in the Department of Family Medicine, James H. Quillen College of Medicine, at East Tennessee State University.

Daniel Blumenthal, MD, MPH, is chair of the Department of Community Health and Preventive Medicine at Morehouse School of Medicine.

Kate Cauley, PhD, is director of the Center for Healthy Communities and an assistant professor in the School of Medicine and School of Professional Psychology at Wright State University.

Richard Christensen, MD, MA, is an assistant professor of psychiatry and director of the Community Mental Health Program at the University of Florida College of Medicine.

Denice Cora-Bramble, MD, is director of the Division of Community Health and an associate clinical professor of health-care sciences at the George Washington University Medical Center.

Diane Demopulos, ARNP, is liaison for the CHAP (Community Health Advancement Program) Saturday Clinic and assistant medical director for the Puget Sound Neighborhood Health Centers.

Sharon A. Dobie, MCP, MD, is an associate professor and CHAP (Community Health Advancement Program) faculty adviser in the Department of Family Medicine at the University of Washington, Seattle.

Amy Driscoll, EdD, was director of community/university partnerships in the Center for Academic Excellence at Portland State University. (Currently she is director for teaching, learning, and assessment at California State University-Monterey Bay.)

Joellen B. Edwards, PhD, RN, is dean and a professor in the College of Nursing at East Tennessee State University.

James E. Florence, DrPH, CHES, is an assistant professor in the College of Public and Allied Health at East Tennessee State University.

Charlene Forslund, MS, is a CHAP (Community Health Advancement Program) educator, and former CHAP student coordinator, at the University of Washington, Seattle.

Paul Freyder, MSW, is executive director of the Public Inebriate Program of the Salvation Army in Pittsburgh.

Deborah Gardner, RN, MSN, is a doctoral student in nursing administration and health-care policy at George Mason University, and an evaluation coordinator for ISCOPES at George Mason University and the George Washington University.

Sherril Gelmon, DrPH, is an associate professor of public health in the College of Urban and Public Affairs at Portland State University and a senior fellow in the Center for the Health Professions at the University of California-San Francisco.

Carol Gentry is chair of the Johnson County Community Partnership Initiative advisory board and a member of the governing board.

Sara Goodman, MEd, was coordinator of elementary teacher preparation at Dartmouth College.

Bruce A. Goodrow, PhD, is a professor in the College of Public and Allied Health at East Tennessee State University.

Doreen Harper, PhD, is an associate professor and director of community partnerships and faculty practice in the College of Nursing and Health Care Sciences at George Mason University.

Catherine A. Heaney, PhD, MPH, is an associate professor in the Division of Health Behavior and Health Promotion, School of Public Health, at the Ohio State University.

William G. Hobson, MA, is executive director of the Downtown Emergency Service Center in Seattle.

Joyce Holl is program administrator for the Program of Health Care to Underserved Populations at the University of Pittsburgh Medical Center.

Barbara Holland, PhD, is vice provost at Northern Kentucky University. Previously, she was associate vice provost at Portland State University.

Betty Holton, RN, is director of health services for the Dayton Public Schools.

Connie Huffine, BA, is CHAP (Community Health Advancement Program) coordinator in the Department of Family Medicine at the University of Washington.

Elvira Jaballas, MD, is medical director of the Wright Patterson Medical Center Pediatrics Partnership and an associate clinical professor in the School of Medicine, Wright State University.

G. Christian Jernstedt, PhD, is a professor of psychology at Dartmouth College.

Mary Jane Kelley, PhD, is an assistant professor in the Section for Medical Education, James H. Quillen College of Medicine, at East Tennessee State University.

Deborah Kippen, MD, was medical director and clinical associate professor of medicine at Pioneer Square Clinic in Seattle.

Meryl S. McNeal, PhD, is a clinical assistant professor in the Department of Community Health and Preventive Medicine at Morehouse School of Medicine.

Beth Morris, MPH, was a member of the HPSISN program evaluation team as a graduate student in public health at Portland State University.

Fred Murphy, MSPH, is executive director of the Southeastern Primary Care Consortium (SPCC) in Atlanta.

Edward O'Neil, PhD, MPA, is executive director of the Center for the Health Professions at the University of California-San Francisco.

Thomas P. O'Toole, MD, was director of the Program of Health Care to Underserved Populations at the University of Pittsburgh Medical Center.

Virginia Reed, MSN, is completing her PhD in evaluation research and has worked for more than 25 years in health-care management and consulting.

JoAnne Rhone, PhD, is a professor in the School of Social Work at Clark-Atlanta University.

Andrew Schamess, MD, MPH, is medical director at La Clinica del Pueblo and an assistant clinical professor of health-care sciences at the George Washington University.

Lorine Spencer, BSN, MBA, is an assistant professor in the School of Nursing at Georgia State University.

Jennifer Sage Smith, MPH, is program coordinator for the C. Everett Koop Institute at Dartmouth College.

Paul E. Stanton, Jr., MD, is vice president for health affairs and dean of the James H. Quillen College of Medicine at East Tennessee State University.

JoEllen Tarallo-Falk, PhD, is a licensed health educator and director of curriculum and assessment for the Windham Southeast Supervisory Union in Brattleboro, Vermont.

Melinda Tonelli, MD, was coordinator of the Dermatology Clinic for the Homeless at the University of Washington, Seattle.

Wanda Vaghan is chair of the Hawkins County Memorial Hospital board and a member of the Hawkins County Community Partnership Initiative advisory board and governing board.

Sheila Virgin, DSN, RN, CS, FNP, is an associate professor in the College of Nursing at East Tennessee State University.

Joy E. Wachs, PhD, RN, is an associate professor in the College of Nursing at East Tennessee State University.

Joseph Walsh, MEd, was coordinator of educational programs for the C. Everett Koop Institute at Dartmouth College.

Series Editor

Edward Zlotkowski is senior associate at the American Association for Higher Education and senior fellow at Campus Compact. He also is professor of English and founding director of the Service-Learning Project at Bentley College.

About AAHE

AAHE's Vision AAHE envisions a higher education enterprise that helps all Americans achieve the deep, lifelong learning they need to grow as individuals, participate in the democratic process, and succeed in a global economy.

AAHE's Mission AAHE is the individual membership organization that promotes the changes higher education must make to ensure its effectiveness in a complex, interconnected world. The association equips individuals and institutions committed to such changes with the knowledge they need to bring them about.

About AAHE's Series on Service-Learning in the Disciplines

Consisting of 18 monographs, the Series goes beyond simple "how to" to provide a rigorous intellectual forum. *Theoretical essays* illuminate issues of general importance to educators interested in using a service-learning pedagogy. *Pedagogical essays* discuss the design, implementation, conceptual content, outcomes, advantages, and disadvantages of specific service-learning programs, courses, and projects. All essays are authored by teacher-scholars in that discipline.

Representative of a wide range of individual interests and approaches, the Series provides substantive discussions supported by research, course models in a rich conceptual context, annotated bibliographies, and program descriptions.

See the order form for the list of disciplines covered in the Series, pricing, and ordering information.

Yes! Send me the following monographs as they are released.

Price per vol. (includes shipping*):   **List** $28.50 ea   **AAHE Member** $24.50 ea

Bulk prices (multiple copies of the *same* monograph only):
10-24 copies $22.50 ea; **25-99 copies** $21.00 ea; **100+ copies** $15.00 ea

	Quantity	Price	Subtotal
Complete Series (all 18 vols.)		$405	
Accounting			
Biology			
Communication Studies			
Composition			
Engineering			
Environmental Studies			
History			
Management			
Medical Education			
Nursing			
Peace Studies			
Philosophy			
Political Science			
Psychology			
Sociology			
Spanish			
Teacher Education			
Women's Studies			

Total _____

Shipping*
Price includes shipping to U.S. destinations via UPS. Call AAHE's Publications Orders Desk at 202/293-6440 x780 if you need information about express and/or foreign delivery.

Payment (F.I.D. #52-0891675)
All orders must be prepaid by check, credit card, or institutional purchase order/number, except AAHE members may ask to be billed.

❑ Bill me; I am an AAHE member. (Provide member # below)
❑ Check payable to "AAHE."
❑ Institutional Purchase Order/Number: #_____
❑ VISA ❑ MasterCard ❑ AmEx

_____
Cardholder's Name (please print)

_____
Cardholder's Signature

_____
Card Number   Exp. Date

Bill This Order To (if "Ship To" address is different, please provide on an attached sheet) :

_____   ___ ___ ___ ___ ___ ___
Name   AAHE Member #

_____
Institution   Address

_____
City   State   Zip

_____
Phone/Email   Fax

Mail/Fax this order to: AAHE Publications, PO Box 98168, Washington, DC 20090-8168; fax 202/293-0073; www.aahe.org. Visit AAHE's website to read excerpts from other volumes in the Series. Need help with your order? Call 202/293-6440 x780.